To Eilidh
with love
from

June 24th 1895.

Listen!

Listen!

Themes from the Bible retold for children
by
A. J. McCallen

Illustrations by
Ferelith Eccles Williams

HarperCollins

HarperCollins*Religious*
a division of HarperCollins*Publishers*
77–85 Fulham Palace Road
Hammersmith, London W6 8JB

Collins Dove
PO Private Bag 200
Burwood, Victoria 3125
Australia

Collins Liturgical New Zealand
PO Box 1, Auckland

First published 1976
Twelfth printing 1993

© text 1976 A. J. McCallen
© illustrations 1976
William Collins Sons & Co. Ltd

Library of Congress Cataloguing-in-Publication Data

McCallen, A.J.
  Listen! : themes from the Bible

  Includes bibliographical references and
  index
  Summary: A collection, arranged by themes,
of stories and songs from the Old and
New Testaments.
  1. Bible stories. English.
(1. Bible stories)   I. Eccles-Williams.
Ferelith. ill. II. Title.
BS 651.2.M38   1987   220.9'505   87-15134
ISBN 0-00-599528-0

Made and printed in Hong Kong

CONTENTS

WE LOVE GOD

We will follow Jesus

We are the family of God

FOREWORD

Teachers recognise the importance of presenting the truths of the faith in a form which is meaningful to the child. The study of themes which relate the teaching of the Church to the world the child understands is one method of achieving this objective. Thematic approaches in religious education, therefore, have been employed in our schools for the past few years. Themes which encourage the child's fuller participation in the liturgy of the Church have been used with notable success in class, school and parish celebrations.

In this book Father McCallen has grouped scripture readings into themes which can be used successfully at morning assemblies, services of prayer and other celebrations. I feel sure that teachers and children will be grateful to him for providing such a book of readings and I commend it to all who are concerned in the religious education of children.

✠ JOHN GERARD
Bishop of Middlesbrough

March 1975

8

PREFACE

The place of the Bible in Christian life and worship – and therefore in a classroom of a church school – is a fundamental one. But it is an adult book, and the questions it deals with are adult questions. If boys and girls, growing up in the Christian community, using and hearing the words of the Bible, are to begin to realise what kind of book they are listening to and so really to listen to it in their own acts of worship and in the classroom, they need special help – simple selections, simple words, simple approaches. This is a most difficult undertaking, demanding sensitiveness to children's ways and thoughts and expert knowledge of what the Bible is really saying.

I am glad to commend *Listen!* I was privileged to see it in its earlier form, and I encouraged Father McCallen to develop it. This book has not just been made *for* children; it has been made *with* them. I am sure that it will be a great help, far beyond the churches and schools for which it was originally prepared, to many children and their teachers.

ALAN DALE
Dartmouth

June 1975

INTRODUCTION

Children,
this is your book.
It was written for you
and I hope you like it.

God our Father has given us a wonderful world.
But that's not all he has done.
He has also given us his Son, Jesus,
to be our teacher and our friend.
Even today we can listen to the stories about Jesus and his
   followers,
and they still sound as good as ever.

You can read through these pages all by yourself.
Or if there are a few of you together,
you can read them out loud and make them into plays.

Enjoy yourselves!

A. J. MCCALLEN

1   GOD IS WISE, GOD IS KIND

God is wonderful – he understands everything. He gives us a wonderful world to live in – an exciting world! and there's so much to see in it.

The Reading comes from the book of a wise man called Ben Sirah.

God must be very wise.

He made every grain of sand on the beach
and there's so many of them
that we could never count them all.

He made every drop of rain that falls from the sky
and we couldn't count them all either.

Look up at the sky
and see how high it is above us!

Go up to the top of a high building
and look how far you can see
(and the land stretches even further away still!)

Go out on the sea in a boat
and look down into the water
and see how deep it is!

God is very, very wise,
and he wants all his friends
to become wise like him.

The world is so good that we want to say 'thank you' to God. Here is a poem from the 'Book of Praise' which does just that.

Thank you, Father,
You are good to us.

You made the sky for us
For you are so wise.

Thank you, Father,
You are good to us.

You made the earth for us
For you are kind.
Thank you, Father,
You are good to us.
You gave the sun to us
To shine all day long.
Thank you, Father,
You are good to us.
You gave the moon to us
To shine through the night.
Thank you, Father,
You are good to us.

*God is certainly wise, but he is also very kind. In fact he has been very good
to all of us, so we must try to be kind to each other, then we will be good
like him. This is what Jesus tells us to do.*

*The Reading comes from the
Gospel of Saint Matthew.*

One day, Jesus said:

God is your Father,
you must behave like his children.

He takes care of everyone
– bad people and good people
honest people and dishonest people.
He treats them all the same.

Look how the sun shines
and the rain falls
on everyone in the same way.

If you are God's children
you must act like God
and take care of each other.

2 🔯 THE WORLD IS GOOD

God made everything for us and he made it all very good!
The Reading comes from the Book of Beginnings.

God said:

Let there be dry land!
(and he called it 'The Earth').

Let there be water round the land!
(and he called it 'The Sea').

Let there be a roof over the land!
(and he called it 'The Sky').

And God said it was good.

God said:

Let there be a light to shine during the day!
(and he called it 'The Sun').

Let there be smaller lights to shine at night!
(and he called them 'the Moon' and 'The Stars').

And God said it was good.

God said:

Let plants grow in the soil
and let there be fruit trees!

Let there be fishes to swim in the sea
and birds to fly in the sky!

Let there be wild animals and tame animals
and all sorts of creeping things!

And God said it was good.

Then God said:

Let us make people,
and he made men and women
and put them in charge of the world.

Then God looked at everything
and God said 'It is all very good!'

✠

*Jesus knew that the world was very good. In fact he liked the world a lot.
He thought it was very beautiful – especially at harvest time.*

The Reading comes from the Gospel of Saint John.

One day Jesus said:

Everything is going just right!
There's going to be a marvellous harvest.

Isn't it wonderful!
One man sows the seeds
and three months later the field is full of golden corn,
ready for the harvest.
Then another man comes and cuts down the corn
and stores it in the barns.
And everyone is happy together.

3 ⊞ FLOWERS ARE BEAUTIFUL

During the Winter most of the flowers stop growing. But in Spring time they begin to come up once more. Each year it is the same! You could almost say the flowers die away in winter and then rise up again in Spring!

The Reading comes from 'The Song of Songs'.

When Winter is finished,
and the rain has stopped falling,
then the plants begin to grow.

The birds sing
and leaves appear on the trees
and at last you can smell the perfume of the flowers.

This is the time to sing for joy!

⊞

The trees look so strong, you would hardly think they changed at all. But they do! Each year they grow new leaves and some trees even grow fruit that you can eat.

This next reading is a poem from 'The Book of Praise' and it's all about some old fruit trees that grew near a river.

Down by the river
Is a good place for trees.
If the water flows near them,
They never grow dry.
Their leaves are not withered,
They stay green and alive.
And each year their branches
Are covered with fruit.

Jesus knew all about plants. He knew how they grow from little seeds that you plant in the ground. The next reading tells a story about some seeds that grew badly and some other seeds that grew well.

The Reading comes from the Gospel of Saint Mark.

One day, when Jesus was down by the sea,
there were so many people around him
that he had to go and sit in a boat
so he could talk to all the people
who were standing on the beach.

One of the stories he told went like this:

'Listen everyone!' he said.

There was once a man who went out to plant some seeds.
As he walked along,
some of the seeds fell on the path
and the birds came and ate them up.

Some of the seeds fell on hard soil,
and they never had a chance.
They had just begun to grow,
when the sun came out and dried them up
– for they had no roots to suck up the water.

Some of the seeds fell on a patch of weeds,
and the weeds choked them
so they couldn't grow properly.

But the man did manage to plant most of the seeds
and he planted them in good soil
just where he wanted.
And they grew and they grew and they grew.

4 ✥ FLOWERS DON'T WORRY ABOUT ANYTHING!

God likes flowers – he thinks they make the world beautiful, and he doesn't want them to be spoilt.

The Reading comes from the book of a Wise Man called Isaiah.

God says:

I am a Gardener,
and I look after my garden
all day and all night.

I keep watering all my plants
because I don't want them to dry up
or their leaves will fall off.

If I find any weeds,
I will pull them up and burn them.

Then the whole of my garden will be filled with flowers.

✥

Jesus liked flowers as well. He knew that his Father took good care of them. That was obvious. But he wanted people to know that God doesn't just take care of the flowers, he takes care of everything – and everyone.

The Reading comes from the Gospel of Saint Matthew.

One day Jesus said:

Look at the flowers!

They don't worry about anything,
and yet they look more beautiful
than a King dressed in his best clothes!

So don't worry about yourselves.
If God takes so much trouble over the flowers
even though they are going to be cut down tomorrow and burnt,
then he will certainly take good care of you.

5 🕂 GOD MAKES EVERYTHING GROW

Harvest is a wonderful time when everyone is happy.
The Reading comes from the Book of Moses.

God said:

If you obey my rules
and do what I ask you to do,
then I will give you all the rain you need,
just at the right time to make things grow.

Everything will grow beautifully in the soil
and the trees will be covered with fruit.

You will be able to harvest your food all the year round
and eat as much as you want.

🕂

Jesus thought it was wonderful
to see the corn growing all by itself.

The Reading comes from the Gospel of Saint Mark.

One day Jesus said:

The farmer goes out
and plants the seeds in his field.
But then he leaves them there
to grow all by themselves.

He doesn't understand *how* they grow
– he only knows they do –
even while he is asleep at night.

All of a sudden a little shoot appears
then it grows larger
and then the corn is there
– all fully grown.

Then Jesus said:
That is the way God works!

6 GOD TAKES CARE OF THE ANIMALS AS WELL

Once upon a time there was a terrible flood and it rained for so long that the whole of the land was covered in deep water.

But God didn't want any of the good people to drown in the floods, so he told a man called Noah to get them all into a boat where they would be safe and dry. Then God told Noah to save all the animals as well for they also had done nothing wrong.

The Reading comes from the Book of Beginnings.

God said to Noah:

Go and find two of each of the birds and the animals
and put them aboard your ship.
Then make sure you have enough food for them
and for everyone else.
So Noah did as he was told
and he took aboard the wild beasts and the cattle
and the animals that crawl on the earth
and the birds that fly in the sky.

⊞

The flood was very bad, but it stopped raining in the end, and the wind began to blow all the water away.

Then Noah sent out a raven
to see if the raven could find dry land.
But it just flew round and round in circles
– there was nowhere dry for it to land.

Then Noah sent out a dove
to see if the dry land had appeared again,
and even the dove could not find anywhere to land.

20

But Noah sent out the dove a second time,
and it came back with an olive branch in its beak.
The next time Noah sent out the dove
it did not come back at all
for it had found dry land at last
and stayed there.

Then God said to Noah:

Come out of your ship
and let all the animals and birds come out as well,
for the flood is finished.

So Noah did what he was told
and he thanked God for saving him from drowning
in the waters of the flood.

*In the story of the Flood, the dove brought back a branch from the olive
tree. In the next reading, we have one of the stories Jesus told, and this
time the birds are resting on the branches of a mustard tree.*

The Reading comes from the Gospel of Saint Mark.

One day Jesus said:

The mustard seed is the smallest seed in the world,
but when you plant it in the ground,
it grows and becomes so big
that the birds can come
and build their nests in the shade of its branches.

Then Jesus said:
God works like that.

21

7 ⊠ THE SHEPHERD AND HIS SHEEP

This first reading is all about looking after sheep. Unless we are shepherds ourselves, we will probably not have a lamb or a sheep at home, but we might have some other kind of animal as a pet. This reading tells us to take good care of it.

The Reading comes from the book of a Wise Man called Ezekiel.

Shepherds should feed their sheep.
They should build them up, if they are weak,
and take care of them when they are sick.

If any of the sheep get lost,
the shepherd should go after them
in case they are left out on the cold mountainside
and the wild animals attack them and kill them.

If you are a good shepherd
you must really look after your sheep.

22

God looks after each of us just as carefully as a good shepherd looks after his sheep.

Jesus is a good shepherd as well and he knows each one of us – even our names. He is certainly not a stranger to us, he is our friend, and we are glad to follow him.

The Reading comes from the Gospel of Saint John.

One day Jesus said:
Sheep listen to their own shepherd
and they will follow him.
He can even call them one by one
for he knows their names
and he can call them out of the sheepfold through the gate.

When they have all come out,
he walks in front of them,
and they all follow
because they know the sound of his voice.

Of course, they would never follow a stranger
because they would not know the sound of his voice.
They would run away from him
if he told them to follow him.

Then Jesus said:

I am a shepherd
and I'm a *good* shepherd.
I know all my sheep, every one of them,
and they know me.

23

8 ✠ SPARROWS DON'T COST MUCH!

Saint John knew that every father loves his child. Sometimes, when our own father is angry with us for doing wrong, we may think that he doesn't love us and will never forgive us. But that's not true – he's probably quite proud of us, even if he is sometimes angry with us.
Saint John says that God is our Father as well, and he loves us all.

The Reading comes from one of the Letters of Saint John.

Dear Friends,

See how much God thinks of us –
he calls us *his children*
and we really are, you know.

God takes care of us
so we must take care of each other.

God loves us
so we must love each other.

If we don't know that
we don't know anything about God our Father,
because 'God *is* Love'.

✠

Jesus must often have seen the little sparrows hopping about on the ground. But even if they are so small, God still looks after them, because 'God is love'.

The Reading comes from the Gospel of Saint Luke.

One day Jesus said:
God does not forget about even the little sparrows.

They are not very important
and they don't cost much to buy,
but God remembers each one of them.

So don't worry about yourself.
God will take good care of you
for you are worth more than all the sparrows in the world.

9 ♢ LET THERE BE LIGHT!

Sometimes it's exciting to be out in the dark, but usually it's rather frightening. You can't see and you bump into things, and it's scarey! Wouldn't it be terrible if there was no light at all and it was always dark!

The Reading comes from the Book of Beginnings.

In the beginning,
the world was all empty,
and everything was dark and gloomy.
But God was there
like the wind that blows over the sea at night.

And God said:
Let there be light!
And there was light!

And the light was wonderful!

♢

People didn't have electric lights, when Jesus was born. They used candles instead. But the candles did the same job and lit up the darkness.

The Reading comes from the Gospel of Saint Matthew.

One day Jesus said:
Do you light a candle
and then cover it over with a bucket?

Of course you don't,
you want it to light up the whole room
so that everyone can see.

Then Jesus said:
If you are good,
you will be like a candle
that shines brightly for everyone to see.

And if they see that you are good
(and they know that you are following God)
then they will know that God is good.

10 ♢ BLIND MEN CAN'T SEE!

It's good to enjoy the sunshine and the daylight, if you can see. But some people are blind and they cannot see the sun at all. They cannot even tell the difference between daylight and darkness. Jesus must have known how terrible it was to be blind. This reading tells the story of a blind man that Jesus cured.

The Reading comes from the Gospel of Saint Luke.

One day
when Jesus and his friends were leaving Jericho,
a blind beggar heard Jesus going by.
Everyone was saying 'It's Jesus of Nazareth!'
So the blind man shouted out to Jesus and said:
'Help me, Jesus!'
Everyone told him to shut up,
but this only made him shout all the louder.

Jesus heard him shouting
and he stopped.
'Bring him here,' he said.
So they did.
'Cheer up,' they told the blind man,
'Jesus wants to see you.'
Then Jesus said:
'What do you want me to do for you?'
And the blind man said:
'Lord, please let me see.'
So Jesus said, 'All right – you trusted me;
You *will* get better!'

And straightaway, the man could see,
and he was able to walk behind Jesus along the road.

✣

It is wonderful to see, and we thank God for it. Here is a prayer of thanks from the Book of Praise. The blind man who came to Jesus might even have said it himself when he was healed.

I love you, my Lord,
for you have made me strong.
I thank you, my Lord,
for you have heard my prayer.

You have been like a light before my eyes.
You have made my darkness into light.

11 ⁂ DON'T TOUCH THE FIRE OR YOU'LL GET BURNT!

If you see a big bonfire burning brightly, you will see how the flames flicker and crackle up into the air. Fire is funny stuff! The flames never stay still – they leap and twist about. And they are so hot that you would burn yourself badly if you touched them.

The Reading comes from the Book of a Wise Man called Isaiah.

It is good to bake bread over a fire.
It is good to sit down in front of it and feel warm.

But the little fire can blaze up
and then no one can bear the heat of its flames,
for it can burn people
as if they were wisps of straw.

⊠

Next we have a story about a farmer who burnt all the weeds in his fields in a great big fire.

The Reading comes from the Gospel of Saint Matthew.

One day Jesus told this story:

Once upon a time there was a farmer
who sowed good seed in his field.
But one night,
a wicked man came and sowed *weeds* in the field
and ran away.

The wheat began to grow beautifully,
but the weeds grew at the same time,
and they were all mixed up with the wheat.

So the man who helped the farmer went to him and said:
'Where have all the weeds come from?
I thought we only sowed good clean seed in that field!'

'I think we have an enemy,' said the farmer,
'and he has planted weeds in our field
just to cause us trouble.'

'Shall we pull out all the weeds now?' said the man,

'No!' said the farmer.
'If you do that,
you may pull up all the wheat as well.
No, leave them as they are,
and at harvest time
we will gather the weeds first
and tie them into bundles
and burn them on the fire.
Then we will be able to collect the wheat safely
and put it into my barn.'

Then Jesus said:
That's how God works as well.

12 ⊞ THE FIRE OF GOD

We cannot see God but we still know he is here with us. He is like the flames of a fire. We can all tell when a fire is burning – even with our eyes shut. We can feel its heat coming towards us even if we cannot see the heat. Even if we sit and watch the flames, we cannot see them properly. They come and go too quickly.

Perhaps that is why God is often said to be like a burning fire – because he is so strong and warm, and yet many people still cannot see him!

The Reading comes from the Book of Moses.

Moses was a shepherd
who lived near the desert.

One day,
he went up Mount Sinai with his sheep
and he saw a bush that seemed to be on fire.
When he came closer to the bush,
he heard the voice of God coming from the blazing flames.
God said: 'Moses!'
and Moses said, 'Yes, Lord, here I am.'
Then God said,
'I am the God of your family,
the God of Abraham, Isaac and Jacob.

'I can see that the Hebrew People are all slaves in Egypt.
But I am going to help you all.
You will escape from Egypt,
and I will give you a beautiful land to live in
and you will have plenty to eat there.'

⊞

Moses felt that God was like a blazing fire because God was strong. Jesus is the same. He also is like a fire, which burns so strongly that everyone can feel his strength and power.

The Reading comes from the Gospel of Saint Luke.

One day Jesus said:
I am like a blazing fire,
and I want everyone else to feel its heat.

13 ꡚ HELP, LORD, WE'RE DROWNING!

Here is a poem from the Book of Praise. It was written by a man who nearly drowned. He must have walked into the river or into the sea, and gone too far. He is scared stiff and prays to God for help.

Save me, O God, I'm drowning!
The water is up to my neck!
I'm standing on soft oozy mud
and my feet are beginning to sink.
I cannot stand up
for the waves push me down,
and the water is getting still deeper.

Save me, O God, I'm drowning!
The mud is sinking below me,
the water is pushing me over!
Save me or I will die!

ꡚ

Water is strong and dangerous, that's why we should always be careful in the sea. It's very easy to get drowned. The next reading tells the story of the time when the followers of Jesus thought they were going to be drowned in a storm at sea.

The Reading comes from the Gospel of Saint Mark.

One night Jesus said to his friends:

'Let's go over to the other side of the lake.'

So they left the big crowds
and got into a boat to go to the other side.
Then suddenly, the wind began to blow,
and big waves splashed into the little boat
so that it started to fill with water.

But Jesus was so tired,
he just lay down with his head on a cushion
and went to sleep.

His friends woke him up, and said,
'Look! We're sinking.
Why aren't you doing something to help?'

So Jesus sat up
and he told the wind to stop making a noise,
and he told the waves to stop rocking the boat.

Suddenly the wind just died away
and the waves became calm again.
Then Jesus turned to his friends and said,

'Why were you so frightened?
You should have known by now
that I would not let you down.'

*Here is another poem from the Book of Praise. The person who wrote
it must have thought that God was asleep – like Jesus in the boat.
Sometimes we may think God has gone to sleep, especially if we
don't get what we ask for. But we can be sure that God is always
ready to help, if we need him.*

Wake up, God!
Don't say you're still sleeping!
Can't you see we need you.
So please don't hide away.
Look! We're all in trouble.
Don't forget us, please.

Stand up, God, and hear us!
Show us that you love us.
Come and help us now.

14 ⊞ WATER, WATER EVERYWHERE, AND NOT A DROP TO DRINK!

Moses and all the People of God escaped from Egypt. They had been slaves – but now they were free, and they were on their way to 'The Promised Land'. But first they had to cross the desert, and everything became hot and sandy. Then they ran out of water.

The Reading comes from the Book of Moses.

They walked for three whole days,
until they had used up all their water.
But when they looked for some more water,
they could only find a pool
where the water was too horrible to drink.

Everyone grumbled at Moses, and said,
'What are we going to drink now?'
So Moses asked God to help him,
and God did not let him down.

Moses found a special kind of wood
that he could put into the water
to make it nice to drink again.
Then everyone could have as much water as they wanted.

Not very long afterwards,
they came to a place
where there were lots of palm trees
and seven pools of clean drinking water,
and so they pitched their tents there and set up camp.

✠

*Even though the People of God were terribly thirsty, they still could not
drink the water in the poisoned pool, until Moses made it good to drink
again. In the next story, Jesus and his friends were very thirsty, but they
couldn't drink the water because it was right down at the bottom of a deep
well.*

The Reading comes from the Gospel of Saint John.

One day Jesus and his friends had to go from Judea to Galilee.
They walked all through the morning until they were tired,
then they came to a place called 'Jacob's Well'
and stopped there for a rest.

Jesus sat down beside the well outside the town,
while his friends went to buy some food,
and as he sat there,
a woman came along with a jug
to get some water from the well.

Jesus asked this woman for a drink.
At first, the woman was surprised that Jesus spoke to her
because she did not know him at all.
But they soon began to talk to each other
and they were still talking
when the others came back with the food.
And she left her jug behind, when she went away,
so they could all have a drink of water from the well.

15 🔁 FOOD, GLORIOUS FOOD!

Everyone enjoys eating. Food is one of the best things that God gives to us. In this reading, we hear the story of Abraham's visitors, who came to see him and stayed for a tasty meal.

The Reading comes from the Book of Beginnings.

One day Abraham was sitting in front of his tent.
It was a hot afternoon
and the sun was high in the sky.

When Abraham looked up,
he saw three men coming towards him.
So he got up and went out to welcome them.

'Come and have something to eat,' he said.
'Come and sit down in the shade of the trees
and I will get you some water
so that you can have a wash.'

Abraham then went back into his tent
and told Sarah, his wife, to bake some bread.
Next he told his servant
to go and get some tasty meat and cook it.
And he went himself to get some milk,
so that he could give his visitors a really good meal.

While they were eating, one of the visitors said,

'Tell your wife
that we will come back in a year's time
and she will have a baby.'
Now Sarah was in the tent and she heard him saying this
and she just laughed,
because she was far too old to have a baby.
But later on Abraham came and told her off.
'God can do anything he wants,' he said,
'and if he wants you to have a baby,
you will!'

36

And, of course, she did.
She gave birth to a little baby boy
and she called him 'Isaac'.

✥

Jesus enjoyed his food and we often hear about him going out for a meal with his friends. In the next reading, he is telling us how to make bread, and he shows us how the yeast makes the flour completely different.

The Reading comes from the Gospel of Saint Matthew.

One day Jesus said:

'When you make bread,
you take a lot of flour
(and some water)
and you mix it all up with a little bit of yeast.

'This little bit of yeast then gets to work on the flour
and it makes it grow and swell up,
until it is all ready for baking.'

Then Jesus said:

'God works like that.'

We all need to eat food or we will starve to death. If we didn't eat anything at all, we would soon become weak, and we could easily become ill.
In the same way, we need Jesus or we will become 'starved' and weak in another way, and then we may even start to do things wrong through our own fault.

The Reading comes from the Gospel of Saint John.

One day Jesus said:

My Father gives you 'bread from Heaven'
and this bread will make you good like him.

Then he said:

I am the 'bread from Heaven'. If you come to me,
you will never be 'hungry'.

Yes, I have come to feed you,
and if you eat my food
you will live with me
and I will live with you.

✂

Jesus comes to feed us when we are 'hungry' for him. But it is not ordinary food he gives to us. He gives himself to us, because he loves us.

The Reading comes from one of the Letters of Saint Paul.

Dear Friends,
At the Last Supper before he died,
Jesus took some bread, saying,
'Father, thank you for giving us this bread to eat.'
Then he broke it up into pieces and said,
'This is me – this is my body.
This is my gift to you.
Remember me,
when you do this in future.'

Later on when the meal was finished,
Jesus took a cup of wine and said,
'This is the cup of friendship
that is filled with my love.
Remember me
when you do this in future.
'Whenever you eat this bread and drink this cup,
let everyone know that I died
for you because I love you.'

17 ✥ IT'S GOOD TO HEAR AND GOOD TO SPEAK

If we could not hear anything or if we couldn't say a single word, life would be very dull! Jesus knew this, so he went out of his way to help people who were deaf and dumb.

The Reading comes from the Gospel of Saint Mark.

One day a man came to Jesus
and he was deaf
(he couldn't speak very well either).

Someone asked Jesus to bless this man
so Jesus told him to come away to somewhere quiet
where there wasn't such a crowd.

Then Jesus touched the man's ears
and put his finger on his tongue,
and said a prayer.

Suddenly the man said, 'I can hear!'
– and he could speak much better as well.

All the people were astonished to see what Jesus could do,
and they said,
'Everything he does is wonderful.'

Perhaps the deaf man who was healed said a prayer like this.

The Reading comes from the Book of a Wise Man called Isaiah.

I want to tell the whole wide world
– 'God has been good to me!'
I want to tell the whole wide world
– 'God is wonderful!'
I want to sing and to shout
because I am so happy
for God has come to me
and he is great!

God is powerful and strong, but he is also kind and gentle. This reading tells us about this gentleness of God for, as Elijah discovers, God can be as gentle as a whispering breeze.

The Reading comes from the Story of the Kings.

Once upon a time there was a man called Elijah
who had an argument with the King.
The King was very angry with Elijah
and Elijah had to escape as fast as he could.
So he tucked up his cloak
and ran away.

Elijah was so frightened
that he went off into the desert
and walked for the whole of a day as far as he could.
Then he sat down under a little bush and said,
'Please let me die, Lord,
I've had enough!'
Then he fell asleep.

When he woke up, he had something to eat and drink
and he felt a lot better.
So he began to walk again
until he came to Mount Sinai,
and he stayed that night
in a cave on the mountainside.

Then God told him to listen very carefully.

First the wind began to blow
and it blew so strongly
that the big rocks came crashing down
and smashed themselves to pieces in the valley below.

But Elijah couldn't hear the voice of God.

Then the mountain began to shake with an earthquake.

But Elijah still couldn't hear the voice of God.

Then a fire broke out on the mountainside,
and the flames from the fire
leaped up into the sky with a loud crackle.

But Elijah still couldn't hear the voice of God.

Then suddenly,
everything became very still,
and Elijah heard the sound of a gentle breeze,
and he shut his eyes
for at last he *could* hear the sound of the voice of God.

Jesus could also be very gentle and he wanted his friends to be gentle with each other. Then they would live in peace.

The Reading comes from the Gospel of Saint John.

One day Jesus said,

'I leave you "PEACE".
I give you my own kind of peace.

'Do not be worried or upset.
do not be afraid.'

19 ⊞ MAKE MUSIC AND PRAISE GOD

Music can make us happy and when we're happy, we praise God much better.

The Reading comes from one of the Letters of Saint Paul.

Dear Friends,

Don't forget that God wants to get to know you,
because he loves you.

But you must help each other
to know how much God loves you
by singing his songs.

And remember!
When you sing these songs,
say 'thank you' to God
for he is your Father in heaven.

⊞

God likes to hear people when they are happy, and the people in the next poem from the Book of Praise are very happy.

God is very good to us
  Let's praise him.

Let's play the trumpet
  Let's praise him.
Let's play the guitar
  Let's praise him.
Let's play the drums
  Let's praise him.
Let's play the violins
  Let's praise him.
Let's play the recorders
  Let's praise him.

Let's crash the cymbals
   Let's praise him.
Let's dance for joy
   Let's praise him.

Let everyone who can breathe praise God!

*Jesus had not been in Jerusalem for quite a long time. So when he did come
back his friends were very glad to see him and, of course, they showed their
happiness as soon as they began to sing.*

The Reading comes from the Gospel of Saint Luke.

When Jesus arrived at the Olive Hill,
a crowd of his friends came out to meet him.
They were very happy,
and began to praise God at the top of their voices,
thanking him for all the wonderful things that Jesus had done.
And they started to sing an old song
that began like this:

'Glory to God in the highest,
and peace to his people on earth.
Blessed is he who comes in the name of the Lord!'

God chooses all of us to do a special job in life. Each job is different, of course, and some people have a more difficult job to do than others. But whatever God wants us to do, he promises to help us to do it well.

The Reading comes from the Book of a Wise Man called Isaiah.

God says:

'I have chosen you.
You are working for me now.

'So do not be afraid.

'I am with you – don't worry!
I am your God,
and I will make you strong.
You can hold my hand
and I will help you.'

⊠

It's good to know that God is interested in us. Here is a poem that says 'Thank you' to God. It comes from the Book of Praise.

Let everyone be happy.
Let everyone be glad.
Let everyone be full of joy
and sing to the Lord, our God.

We thank you, God, we praise you, God,
for you are good and loving.

We know the Lord is God,
he gives us life and breath,
for we are his own family
and we belong to him.

We thank you, God, we praise you, God,
for you are good and loving.

God our Father chose Mary to be the Mother of Jesus, and when he asked her to do this for him she said 'Yes – I'll do anything you want!'

The Reading comes from the Gospel of Saint Luke.

One day
God sent his Messenger
to a town called Nazareth
to a girl called Mary
who was engaged to a man called Joseph.

The Messenger said,
'Rejoice, Mary,
for the Lord has blessed you,
and he is with you now!'

Mary didn't know what to say
and she wondered what this meant.
But the Messenger said:
'Do not be afraid –
God is very pleased with you.

'Listen!
You are going to have a baby,
and you will call him Jesus.'

Then Mary said:
'I am the servant of God,
I am glad to do
whatever he wants!'

21 ✠ WAITING FOR JESUS

Jesus is so good that he is like a bright light which lights up the path we must walk on our way to God the Father.

The Reading comes from the Book of a Wise Man called Isaiah.

Once upon a time, everyone lived in the dark
but now – we can see!
They used to live in a world that was full of shadows
but now – we have a light to light up our way!

We have God with us
and he has made us happy.
He has sent us a baby
who is to be our King,
and he will keep everyone safe.

✠

John the Baptist was a very great leader, but Jesus was even greater still.

The Reading comes from the Gospel of Saint Luke.

Lots of people came to John the Baptist and said:
'What have we got to do?'

John said:
'Share things with each other,
and don't be greedy either!'

Everyone thought John was going to be the Great King,
and they all began to get excited.
But John said:
'I am not the Great King that God has promised to send.
Someone else is coming after me,
and he is much more important than I am.

'In fact he is so great
that I am not even good enough
to untie his shoe-laces!'

Jesus comes to help us all.

The Reading comes from one of the Letters of Saint Paul.

Dear Friends,

When the right time came,
God the Father sent Jesus to us.

Jesus had a mother just like the rest of us
and he had to do as he was told – like us.

He wanted to help us all,
and he came to give us the chance
to become the 'Children of God',
so that we could call God 'our Father' – like him.

✠

This is the story of the birth of Jesus in Bethlehem.

The Reading comes from the Gospel of Saint Luke.

Joseph lived in the town of Nazareth
but one day he had to go all the way to Bethlehem with Mary
even though she was going to have a baby.

While they were in Bethlehem,
the baby was born
– it was Mary's first little boy,
and she dressed him up in baby clothes
and made a bed for him in a stable
because there was no room left for them at the Inn.

23 ✠ THE SHEPHERDS COME TO JESUS

Each morning the Sun rises in the sky and fills the world with daylight. Jesus is like that as well – only he fills the world with happiness and goodness.

The Reading comes from the Book of a Wise Man called Isaiah.

In the beginning,
the world was filled with darkness
and it was as black as night.
But God came and changed all that!
He filled the world with his light instead,
just like the sun that shines in the sky every morning.

✠

The shepherds saw a light in the sky that made the night as bright as the day. This is the story of how they discovered that God had sent his Son to visit his family on earth.

The Reading comes from the Gospel of Saint Luke.

Jesus was born in Bethlehem – in a stable,
because there was no room for him at the Inn.

This happened at night time,
and as usual the shepherds were out in the fields
looking after their sheep.

But suddenly, the sky was filled with light,
and they saw the Messenger of God!
At first they were afraid.
But then the Messenger said:
'Do not be afraid!
I have some Good News for you
and for everyone else as well.
Jesus, the Lord, has been born this very night.
You will find him wrapped in baby clothes
and lying in a stable in Bethlehem.'

50

Then the shepherds could hear the sound of many people singing:
'Glory to God in the highest,
and peace to his people on earth!'

The shepherds didn't waste a minute.
They quickly found the stable,
they found Mary and Joseph and the baby,
and they told them everything they had heard.
Mary listened carefully to their story
and she kept all these things in her mind.

Then the shepherds went back to their sheep
thanking God for everything they had seen and heard.

Jesus was born in a small town, and you would hardly have thought that anyone would have taken any notice of what had happened there.
But they did.
People came from far away to bring their presents to him.

The Reading comes from the Gospel of Saint Matthew.

When Jesus was born in Bethlehem
he received a visit from some Wise Men.

First they came to Jerusalem
and they said to King Herod:
'Where will we find the baby
who is the King of the Jews?'

King Herod didn't like this
(he didn't want anyone to be King
except himself!)
But he asked the Priests and the Teachers
if they knew anything about it,
and they said:

'A long time ago
God spoke to the People of Bethlehem like this:

    "I promise you,
    the Great King will be born
    in Bethlehem.
    He will look after you
    like a shepherd who looks after his sheep.
    He will take care of you.
    He will never let you down,
    for he will be the King of the World!" '

So King Herod sent his visitors off to Bethlehem.
'You find the baby,' he said.
'Then come back
and tell me where I can find him,
and I will go and see him as well.'

So the Wise Men went to Bethlehem
and they found Jesus there
with his mother, Mary,
and they gave him their presents.

But they didn't trust King Herod,
and they didn't go back to him.

25 ✠ SIMEON AND ANNA

*If we do wrong, then it is just as if we had run off into the dark away
from the light, so that we cannot see where we are going, and we stumble
and fall down.*

The Reading comes from one of the Letters of Saint John.

Dear Friends,

God is light!
If we do wrong,
we turn away from the light of God
and go off into the dark.

Some people think they can be close to God
and still do wrong.
But they are making a mistake!
The light of God shines on us
to help us do things right
and be happy with everyone.

✠

*Old Simeon and Anna were very glad to see Jesus, and they gave thanks
to God for letting them see 'The Light of the World'.*

The Reading comes from the Gospel of Saint Luke.

The Bible says:
'The first boy that is born in each family
belongs to God,
and the baby's parents must offer their child back to God.'

So when Jesus was born,
Joseph and Mary took him to the Temple in Jerusalem,
and offered him to God
as the Bible told them to do.

When they came to the Temple,
they met an old man called Simeon.
Simeon was a good man
and the Holy Spirit was very close to him.
And as soon as he saw Jesus,
he took him in his arms, and said:

'Thank you, God our Father.
Now I am happy to die,
for I have seen Jesus, the Light of the World!'

Then he blessed Joseph and Mary
for they were standing beside him,
listening to everything he said,
even though they didn't understand what he meant.

There was also an old woman called Anna in the Temple.
She was always there.
She spent the whole day saying her prayers.
When she saw Jesus
she also thanked God
and told everyone
that Jesus would do many great and wonderful things
when he grew up.

Mary and Joseph did everything they were supposed to do
   in the Temple
then they went back to Galilee
and went home to Nazareth.

26 ✠ JESUS GOES TO THE TEMPLE SCHOOL

*When Jesus was born, children learnt most of their lessons by heart –
there were very few books. So in the Jewish schools – and in the Temple
School – the children would sit round the teacher in a circle, and they
would repeat what the teacher said until they had learnt it perfectly.
Here is a poem that Jesus probably learnt in this way – it was an easy
poem to learn because each line begins with a different letter of the
alphabet.*

ALL the world praises you, O Lord,
BECAUSE you have done so many great things.
CAN anyone be as strong as you!
DO not forget us, come now and help us.
EVERYONE knows that you are kind,
FOR you are God our Father.

✠

*Jesus once went to the Temple school for three days, and he joined the
other boys there, until his Mother and Father found him and took him
home.*

The Reading comes from the Gospel of Saint Luke.

On one day of each year
Mary and Joseph went up to the Temple in Jerusalem.

One year, when Jesus was twelve,
they took him with them as well,
and when everything was finished,
Jesus stayed behind in the city,
and his parents went home without him.

Mary and Joseph thought he was with the other children,
and they only found out that he had disappeared
when night-time came.

So they went all the way back to Jerusalem
and looked for him everywhere.

After three days of looking,
they found him at last in the Temple school
with the other children.
He was listening to the teachers
and asking questions.
All the teachers thought he was very clever.

Mary was very glad to see him again,
but she asked him what he'd been doing,
and told him how much they'd been worried.

Jesus told them he was sorry,
but then he said
'All the same you shouldn't have been worried,
you should have known I'd be here in my Father's house.'
Mary and Joseph didn't understand what he meant.

However, he went back to Nazareth again with them,
and he grew up there.
He became tall and strong and wise
for God the Father took good care of him.

27 ✠ JESUS IS BAPTISED

This is the story of the Baptism of Jesus, and it reminds us how much God the Father loves his Son.

The Reading comes from the Gospel of Saint Mark.

One day,
Jesus went to the River Jordan
to see John the Baptist,
and he asked John to baptise him
in the river there.

When Jesus came up out of the water
he saw the Holy Spirit
who came to him like a dove from the sky,
and God the Father said,
'You are my Son and I love you.'

✠

God the Father loves Jesus very much – that's obvious. But he will also love us just the same – if we do what Jesus tells us to do.

The Reading comes from the Gospel of Saint John.

One day Jesus said,

I have always done what my Father has told me,
for I am very close to him
and my Father loves me very much.

I love all of *you* like that,
and I want you to stay close to me
and never go away from me.

If you love me
I know you will do as I say
and my Father will love you.

Yes, my Father and I will come to you
and stay with you.

58

28 ✠ JESUS AND 'THE TWELVE'

This is the story of the day when Jesus asked Peter, Andrew, James and John to come and work with him.

The Reading comes from the Gospel of Saint Mark.

One day,
Jesus was walking down by the sea,
and he saw Peter and his brother Andrew
throwing their nets into the sea,
for they were fishermen.

'Come with me,' said Jesus,
'and I will show you how to fish for men!'

So they left their fishing nets,
and went with Jesus.

Further on,
Jesus saw James and his brother, John.
They were putting their fishing nets into their boat
– they were getting ready to go out fishing.
And Jesus called them as well.

So they left their father and his men in the boat
and followed Jesus straightaway.

⊞

*There were lots of people who followed Jesus and listened to him but his
special friends were called 'The Twelve'.*

The Reading comes from the Gospel of Saint Mark.

Jesus picked out twelve men.
He asked them to come and work with him,
and they said 'Yes'.

He showed them how to tell people about God
and how to make sick people better again.

Here are 'The Twelve' and some of their 'Nicknames':

Simon 'the Rock' (or 'Peter' as we call him).
James and John, the sons of Zebedee,
    who were called 'Thunder and Lightning'.
Andrew, Philip and Bartholomew,
Matthew and James, the son of Alphaeus,
Thomas and Thaddeus,
Simon, the 'Rebel',
and Judas, the man from Kerioth.

29 ☒ JESUS GOES BACK TO NAZARETH

We don't hear much about the family of Jesus except for his Mother, Mary, and Joseph, his Foster-Father. This next reading tells the story of the day when Jesus went home to Nazareth and is one of the few times we hear about them.

The Reading comes from the Gospel of Saint Mark.

One day
Jesus went back to his home town with his friends,
and on the Saturday
he went to the Meeting House
to talk to the people there.

A lot of people came to hear him
and everyone was surprised to hear him speaking so well.
'Isn't he clever!' they said,
'and doesn't he do some wonderful things!'

'Where does he get it all from?
He's only the carpenter, isn't he?
We know his family –
   James and Joseph
   and Jude and Simon,
and his sisters all live here as well.'
But even though they thought he was very clever
they wouldn't believe what he told them.

62

Jesus must have been sad to find that the people of Nazareth didn't believe his teaching. It even seems that some of his own family didn't either.

But there are other people who do. In the next reading Saint Paul tells us that Jesus has another family – the family of all his followers, who have been chosen by God the Father to be the new brothers and sisters of his Son.

The Reading comes from one of the Letters of Saint Paul.

Dear Friends,

God the Father has done many good things for us,
but the best thing he ever did
was to give us his Son, Jesus.

Now that we have Jesus with us,
God has decided to make *us* his sons as well.
So in future,
we must try extra hard to be good,
for we would not like him to see us doing wrong.

Here is a story which shows us how much Jesus liked to meet children.
The Reading comes from the Gospel of Saint Mark.

People often used to bring children to Jesus
and when they did,
Jesus always gave them his blessing.

One day, however,
some of the friends of Jesus told the children to go away.

Jesus was angry when he saw this happening,
and he said:
'Don't stop the children from coming to me.
Don't send them away like that!
Bring them back.'

Then he put his arms round the children
and he blessed them.

⊞

Many of us first came to Jesus when we were baptised as babies. This reading reminds us that we are all children of God, because God has made us clean and good so that we could be part of his family.

The Reading comes from the Book of a Wise Man called Ezekiel.

God says:

I want all my People to come back home
and live with me again.

Your hearts have become as hard as stone,
but I will make you kind
and you will do what I tell you,
for I will give you my holy spirit.

I will pour water over you
and wash all the dirt away
so that you may be clean all over.

You will be my family
and I will be your Father.

In this story Jesus heals a little girl because her father goes to Jesus and asks him to come and help.

The Reading comes from the Gospel of Saint Mark.

One day a man called Jairus came to Jesus
and threw himself down in front of him.
'My little girl is dying,' he said.
'Come and hold her in your arms
and she will get better again.'
So Jesus went along with him.

Then someone came and said.
'It's no use bothering Jesus any more.
Your little girl has just died.'

But Jesus took no notice,
and said to Jairus,
'Don't worry.
All you have to do is to trust me.'

When they got to Jairus' house,
there were lots of people there,
and they were all crying.
So Jesus said,
'What's all this for?
The little girl isn't dead,
She's only asleep.'
But no one believed him,
in fact they even laughed at him.

So Jesus sent everyone
out of the house,
then he went into the room
where the little girl was lying,
and he took with him
only her mother and father,
and Peter, James and John.

Then he held the girl's hand, and said,
'Get up, little girl.'
And she did
and walked round the room!
Her father and mother were so surprised,
they just didn't know what to do,
so Jesus told them to give the girl something to eat.

✣

*After Jesus had died, his followers were able to do the same kind of
things that Jesus himself had done. In this story, Saint Paul heals a
young boy – just as Jesus had healed the little girl.*
*Paul and his friends travelled all over the world to tell people about Jesus.
One day Paul stayed for a week at a place called Troas. And Saint Luke
tells us this story about what happened there.*

The Reading comes from the Story of the Apostles.

On Sunday night,
we met in a big room right at the top of our house
so that we could share the Jesus Meal.
Paul was going away again on the next day,
so he gave us a long talk.
In fact he went on talking all night
until it became too dark to see and we had to light the lamps.

Now there was a young lad there,
sitting on the window ledge,
and he became so tired that he fell asleep
and dropped out of the window
down on to the ground outside.

Someone picked him up
but everyone said he was dead,
everyone, except Paul!

Paul came down and picked the boy up in his arms and said:
'Don't worry, he'll live!'
Then he went back upstairs
and finished off what he was saying!
And the boy *was* all right, and he was able to go home afterwards
    with his parents.

32 ✠ JESUS LOOKS AFTER A LITTLE BOY

People came to Jesus because they trusted him, they knew he could help them.

The Reading comes from the Gospel of Saint Mark.

One day, while Jesus was talking,
a man came up and said,
'My son has fits – can you help him?
He grinds his teeth
and falls down and lies very still on the ground.'
So Jesus said,
'Bring him here.'

When the boy was brought to Jesus,
he had one of these fits.
He threw himself down on the ground,
and began to roll about in a horrible way.

'How long has this been happening?' asked Jesus.
'Since he was a baby,' replied the man.
'Please help him if you can.'

So Jesus said a prayer
and told the boy that his sickness would go away.

Then suddenly the boy gave a scream,
and fell down.
He became so very still
that everyone thought he was dead!

But Jesus picked him up
and helped him to stand up straight,
and the boy was perfectly all right again.

✠

*Peter was like Jesus – he wasn't very rich, but he went round doing good.
And everything he did was done for the sake of Jesus.*

The Reading comes from the Story of the Apostles.

One afternoon,
Peter and John went up to the Temple in Jerusalem,
and while they were there,
they saw someone carrying a man on a stretcher.
This man had never been able to walk,
and each day someone carried him to the Temple Gate
and left him there to beg for money.

When he saw Peter and John,
he asked them for some money.
Peter said, 'I have no money to give you,
but I will help you.
I order you in the name of Jesus,
get up and walk!'
And he took the man's hand
and helped him to stand up.

Suddenly the man's feet and ankles became stronger,
and he did get up and began to walk.
So he went into the Temple with Peter and John
jumping up and down as he went along
praising God in front of everyone!

33 ⊞ JESUS LOOKS AFTER THE PEOPLE WHO FOLLOW HIM

God the Father took care of his People while they were in the desert by making sure they had enough to eat when they were hungry.

Moses knew that he was leading his People to a land where there was plenty to eat, but first they had to go through a desert, and in the desert there was nothing to eat at all.

The Reading comes from the Book of Moses.

The People of God became very hungry in the desert,
so they complained to God.
'We are hungry!' they said,
'We want something to eat!'

God heard them, of course,
and he made sure they did get enough to eat.

Next morning there was a white powder on the ground
– it looked just like frost.
At first no one knew what it was,
but then Moses told them.
'This is the food that comes from God,' he said,
so they gathered together as much as they needed.

They used to grind this powder until it was very fine,
and became like flour.
Then they cooked it
and made it into pancakes.

❸

Jesus also takes care of the people who follow him, and he gives them food to eat just as his Father had done. (Although Saint Luke does not tell us this, the five loaves and the two fishes really belonged to a young boy who was brought along to Jesus by Saint Andrew.)

The Reading comes from the Gospel of Saint Luke.

One day,
Jesus tried to get away with his friends
to a quiet place all by themselves.
But the crowds of people found out where he was going
and they followed him.

So Jesus made them welcome again,
and began to talk to them as usual,
and they brought their sick friends to him.

When evening came,
'the Twelve' wanted Jesus to send all the people back home.
'Send them to the nearest town,' they said,
'so they can find something to eat for themselves
and a place to stay.'

But Jesus said:
'Why don't *you* give them something to eat?'

'But we've only got five loaves and two fishes,' they said,
'Surely you don't expect us to go and *buy* something
for all these people!'

Jesus simply said:
'Let the people sit down.'
And when they had done so,
he took the loaves of bread and the fishes.
He blessed them,
he broke them into pieces,
and gave them to his friends
who gave them to the people in the crowd,
and they all had enough to eat.

Jesus was very brave. He didn't run away and hide, even though he knew that some people wanted to kill him.

The Reading comes from the Gospel of Saint Mark.

One day,
Jesus and his friends were walking along the road
and he suddenly said,
'Who do people think I am?'

His friends said,
'Some people think you are John the Baptist!
And other people think you are one of the great teachers!'

Then Jesus said,
'Who do *you* think I am?'
And Peter said,
'You are the Great King that God promised to send to us.'

After that,
Jesus began to tell his friends
that the Priests and the Teachers were not going to listen to him.
They would kill him instead.
But then God the Father would raise him back to life again.

Peter said,
'This will never happen to you, Jesus!'
But Jesus said,
'You are wrong, Peter!
If you say that, you are not on God's side.'

Sometimes, things go wrong and we feel sorry for ourselves – especially if we have been hurt.
That's a good time to remember that Jesus suffered a lot more than we do, and we can be sure that he will understand all our troubles if we go to him.

The Reading comes from one of the Letters of Saint Paul.

Nothing could be better than knowing Jesus!
I would give up everything,
just to stay friends with him.

Remember how much he suffered
and don't forget
that we can always share our troubles with him
when things go wrong.

Jesus came back to Jerusalem even though he knew some people wanted to get rid of him. Most of the ordinary people thought he was wonderful. He was their King! But Jesus didn't want to be a King of war and fighting, he wanted to be the King of love and peace.

The Reading comes from the Gospel of Saint Matthew.

When they arrived at the Olive Hill,
Jesus said to two of his friends,
'If you go into that village over there,
you will find a donkey and its foal, just as you go in.
Untie them and bring them here.
If anyone asks you who they are for,
tell them they're for me,
and I will send them back as soon as I can.'

So off they went
and they brought back the donkey and the foal
with their coats spread over the animals' backs,
and Jesus then got on.
Some people even put their coats on the ground
in front of Jesus.
Others cut branches off the trees
and put them on the ground for Jesus to ride over.

There were lots of people,
walking in front of Jesus
and walking behind him,
and they all shouted
'Hosanna, Hosanna!
Blessed is he who comes
in the name of the Lord!
Hosanna, Hosanna!'

As Zechariah said:

Everyone shouts – 'Here is the King!'
Everyone is happy, for he is strong
and gentle as well
for he rides on a donkey and her foal!

36 ⊠ THE LAST SUPPER

Moses and all the People of God had to leave Egypt quickly. The King of Egypt had only just said they could go, and they were afraid he would change his mind again. So they had a good meal before they began their long journey.

A Reading from the Book of Moses.

Each family took a sheep or a goat and killed it.
Then they used its meat for the meal.
If any family was too small to eat a whole sheep,
they had to share it with another family.
The animal was roasted over a fire – it had to be well cooked,
and if there was anything left over, it had to be burnt.
There was also unleavened bread to eat
and sauce to go with the meat.

No one sat down for this meal,
they all ate standing up,
for everyone was in a hurry to escape from Egypt.

⊠

This is the story of the Last Supper.

Each year, the Jews had a 'Pass-over Meal', when they ate the 'Pass-over Lamb', and remembered how they had escaped from Egypt long, long ago. The Last Supper was a special meal like this.

The Reading comes from the Gospel of Saint Mark.

The friends of Jesus came to him and said,
'Where do you want us to have the "Pass-over Meal"?'

So Jesus said,
'Go into the city of Jerusalem,
and find the man with the water jug.
Follow him
and he will take you to a house
where you can get a room.
Just tell the owner of the house what I want,
and he will show you a large dining-room upstairs.
Everything will be ready there.'

So they went into the city as he told them to do,
and they found everything just as Jesus had said.

That evening, while Jesus was eating with 'The Twelve',
he said,
'One of you is going to let me down
even though he is sitting with me now!'

They were all very upset,
and each of them asked,
'Surely, Lord, you don't mean me?'
But he said,
'Yes, it is one of you.
and even now, he is still eating with me from the same dish!'

Then he took some bread,
he said the prayer of blessing,
he broke the bread into pieces,
and gave it to them all.
'Take this,' he said,
'This is my body.'
Then he took the cup of wine,
he said the prayer of thanks,
he passed the cup round to them
and they all drank from it.
'This is my life-blood,' he said,
'which will be poured out for you.'

Then they sang a hymn together,
and they went out to the Olive Hill.

Jesus often went away on his own to a quiet place where he could be alone with God the Father during the night.

The Reading comes from the Gospel of Saint Mark.

After the Last Supper,
Jesus went to pray in a quiet place on the Olive Hill,
and he took with him Peter, James and John.

He was very unhappy.
'I am afraid of what is going to happen to me,' he said.
'Don't go away, stay here.'
Then he walked away on his own a little bit.

He fell down on the ground and began to pray to his Father.
'Father, something terrible is going to happen!
Please don't let it happen to me!
I know you can stop it, for you can do anything.'
Then he said,
'Father, if you want it to happen this way,
I will do what *you* want – not what *I* want.'

When he came back,
he found Peter, James and John fast asleep,
'Simon Peter, why are you asleep?' he said.
'Couldn't you stay awake with me for an hour?'

Then he went back again
and said the same prayer once more.

When he came back a second time,
he found them asleep again.
Their eyes were very heavy,
and they just didn't know what to say to him.

When he came back the third time, he said,
'Wake up! Judas is coming now!'
And while he was still talking,
one of his friends, called Judas,
came up with some soldiers,
all armed with swords and clubs.
Judas came right up to Jesus and said,
'Master!'
and kissed him.

Then the soldiers arrested Jesus,
and took him away.

✠

*Jesus was put in prison – so were Peter and John! They discovered that if
you follow Jesus you'll often find it's a hard and difficult thing to do.*

The Reading comes from the Story of the Apostles.

One day, Peter and John went to the Temple
to tell the people there all about Jesus.
There were a lot of people standing round them both
when the Priests and the Temple soldiers came along.
They didn't like the people listening to Peter and John
and so they put them both in prison,
and kept them there all night.

Next morning,
the Priests and the Teachers
made Peter and John stand in front of them
while they asked them questions.
'Who told you to do this?' they asked.

So Peter spoke up,
'I'm very glad to tell you,' he said.
'It was Jesus of Nazareth – the man you killed!
We are doing what *he* told us to do.'

This is the story of how Jesus died.

The Reading comes from the Gospel of Saint Mark.

Jesus was taken to the Governor, Pontius Pilate.
The Governor said he would set Jesus free,
but the people outside shouted,
'Kill him! Kill him!'

So the Governor let the soldiers take Jesus away,
and they hit him in the face
and spat at him.
Then they made him walk to the Hill of the Skull.

On the way they met Simon from Cyrene in Africa
and made him help Jesus to carry his cross.

When they came to the Hill of the Skull,
the soldiers fastened Jesus to the cross.
Then the people came up and made fun of him.

Jesus hung there a long time,
then he shouted out a prayer.
'Father, why have you left me on my own?' he said.
'You seem to be so far away!
Come quickly and help me.
For you are good
and I know you will never let me down.'
Then Jesus died.

The Captain of the soldiers saw all this happen
and he said,
'This man really was the Son of God!'
✠
Not very far away stood some of the women who looked after
Jesus and they saw all this happen as well.

Later on that night,
a man called Joseph asked the Governor
    if he could bury Jesus.
And when the Governor said yes,
Joseph placed the body in a cave,
and put a great boulder in the doorway.

✝

Jesus died, but that was not the end of the story. God the Father raised him back to life again.

The Reading comes from the Story of the Apostles.

One day Peter said,
'Listen, everyone, to what I have to say!

'As you all know,
you killed Jesus of Nazareth,
even though he had done many wonderful things for you.

'But God the Father has raised him from the dead.
He is alive again
and we have seen him!'

Jesus was dead – but now he is alive again!

The Reading comes from one of the Letters of Saint Paul.

Dear Friends,

Jesus died – he was killed!
But God the Father has raised him to life again.

He has made Jesus the King of the World,
and put him in charge of everything.
In fact God the Father
has made him greater than everybody else.

This is the story of what happened on Easter Sunday morning.

The Reading comes from the Gospel of Saint Mark.

On Sunday morning, very early,
– just as the sun was beginning to shine –
Mary Magdalen, Salome, and Mary, the mother of James,
went to the cave where Jesus was buried.

When they got there,
they found the great boulder had been rolled away from the door,
and when they went inside,
they found a young man there, dressed all in white.
At first they were afraid, when they saw him,
so he said,
'Don't be frightened!
You want Jesus who was killed, don't you?
Well, you can see where they put him,
but he's not here now.
He is alive!

'Go and tell Peter and the others
   they will see him in Galilee!'

Then the women came out of the cave,
but they were so frightened,
they ran away as fast as they could
without saying a word to anybody!

This is the story of a journey to a little town near Jerusalem, and it tells how two of his friends met Jesus on the way there.

The Reading comes from the Gospel of Saint Luke.

On Easter Sunday morning,
two of the followers of Jesus
had to go to a place called Emmaus,
and as they walked along, they talked about Jesus,
about what he had said, and how he had died.

While they were talking,
Jesus himself came and joined them,
only they didn't see it was Jesus.

The stranger asked them both what they were talking about,
and they replied,
'Don't you know about Jesus?
We all thought he was going to be our King,
but then he was killed three days ago.
Now even his body has disappeared.
Two of the women we know went to his grave
and they told us it had disappeared!
They said that Jesus was alive again!'

Then Jesus said,
'You just don't seem to understand!
Can't you see that he *had* to suffer and die like that.
It was the only way he could win!'
And he began to explain how the Bible
had said that all these things would happen.

When they came to Emmaus,
the two friends asked the stranger to stay for a meal,
for it was getting dark.

So Jesus went in with them,
and when they sat down at the table,
he took the bread,
he blessed it,
he broke it into pieces
and gave it to them to eat.

And all of a sudden they saw that it was Jesus himself!

A lot of people saw Jesus after he had been raised to life again. That's one way we know he is still alive now.

The Reading comes from one of the Letters of Saint Paul.

Dear Friends,

Jesus died
and he was buried.
But God the Father raised him up to life again.

After this, many people saw Jesus.
First Peter saw him,
next 'The Twelve',
then five hundred people all at the same time!
Then James and all the others.
and last of all
   I saw him as well.

41 DOUBTING THOMAS!

After Jesus had died, God the Father raised him to life again, and most of his friends were able to see him once more for a short time. When they first saw him, some of them were so surprised they thought he was a ghost and were afraid of him. But Jesus really was alive again and he was certainly not a ghost. In fact once he even ate some grilled fish in front of them just to prove it!

The Reading comes from the Gospel of Saint John.

On the Sunday after Jesus had died,
Mary of Magdala came to his followers and said,
'I have seen Jesus!'

Then on the evening of the same day,
Jesus came and showed himself to them all.
It happened like this.

Some of the followers of Jesus were sitting together talking.
They had locked the door behind them
because they were afraid they might be arrested like Jesus.
But Jesus just came straight in and said 'Hello!'
'Peace be with you,' he said,
and he showed them the wounds on his hands and his side.
It was great to see him again.

Then Jesus said,
'My Father has sent me to you.
Now I am sending you to help others.
I give you the Holy Spirit
   to help you to do this.'
And he breathed on them.

'In future,' he said,
'If you forgive people,
I will forgive them as well.'

Thomas the twin wasn't there when Jesus came the first time,
and when he came back they told him
'We have seen Jesus!'
But he said,
'I will not believe it,
until I see him for myself!'
One week later,
Jesus came to them all a second time,
and he said to Thomas,
'Look! here are my hands, hold them!
Feel the wounds on my side as well!'
And Thomas said,
'You are my Lord and my God!'

Then Jesus said,
'You know that I am alive
   because you can see me.
May God bless all those people
   who will not be able to see me
   but will still believe in me!'

42 ✠ JESUS GOES BACK TO HIS FATHER

This is the story of the last time that Jesus was seen by his friends.
The Reading comes from the Gospel of Saint Luke.

Jesus took his friends to the Olive Hill outside Jerusalem.
and he gave them his blessing there.

Then he went away back to his Father,
and they didn't see him any more.

His friends went back again to Jerusalem.

But they were no longer sad.
They were full of joy.

✠

*The followers of Jesus could not see their Lord any more, but they were
not sad – because they knew that he was still alive and they were quite
sure that he was still going to help them.*

*Here is a poem from the Book of Praise – it is a prayer of thanks. Perhaps
the followers of Jesus said this prayer when they went to the Temple each
day.*

We praise the Lord,
for he guides us along the right path.
By day and by night
he shows us what to do.
We shall not fall down
if he is there beside us.

Lord we are happy
for we are safe with you.

43  JESUS SENDS THE HOLY SPIRIT

Before he died, Jesus promised to send us the Holy Spirit.
The Reading comes from the Gospel of Saint John.

Jesus said, 'I am going to leave you soon,
for I am going back to my Father.
But I will not leave you alone,
I will send someone to help you.

'You will not be able to see me,
but you will have my Holy Spirit
to help you and guide you.'

About seven weeks after Jesus had died, some of his friends came back to
Jerusalem for the Jewish feast of Pentecost.
The Reading comes from the Story of the Apostles.

The followers of Jesus were sitting together in one room,
when suddenly
they heard the sound of a strong wind
blowing right through the whole house,
and they could see something like flames of fire everywhere,
that came and touched each one of them.

In this way, they were all filled with the Holy Spirit.

At once they went outside,
and began to tell everyone
the story of Jesus.
There were people there
from every country
in the world,
and they *all* heard
the good news of Jesus!

Jesus promises to come back again as the King of the World.

The Reading comes from one of the Letters of Saint Paul.

Dear Friends,

We are all waiting for Jesus to come back again
from his Father in heaven.

When he does, he will make everything different!
He will make *us* just like himself!

So do not give up.
Keep on doing what Jesus told you to do.

✠

This is a poem about the greatness of the King of all the Earth. It comes from the Book of Praise.

Clap your hands and shout for joy,
God is King of all the earth!

Play the trumpet loud and clear,
God is King of all the earth!

Sing and praise him, everyone,
God is King of all the earth!

Praise him now with all your skill,
God is King of all the earth!

Jesus tells us to keep on being brave and not to be afraid whatever happens to us.

The Reading comes from the Gospel of Saint Mark.

One day, Jesus said,

'Lots of things will go wrong,
and people will hurt you,
but don't be afraid!

'In the end,
you will see me again.
I will come back,
and you will see that I am the King of the world.

'Then I will send out my messengers
    all over the earth,
and I will bring all my friends together,
and they will be happy with me for ever.'

45 ⊞ JESUS TELLS US WHAT TO DO

The first thing that Jesus teaches us is this: God is our Father and he loves us.

The Reading comes from one of the Letters of Saint John.

Dear Friends,

God our Father shows how much he loves us
by sending his Son, Jesus, to live with us.

Listen carefully!
I am not talking about the way *we* love God.
I am talking about the way *God* loves us!
He loves us a lot – he must do,
or he would never have sent Jesus to us.

And now that Jesus has come,
God will forgive all the things we have done wrong.

⊞

If we are going to follow Jesus, we must really try to be good. This is the simple message of this poem from the Book of Praise.

We will not do wrong,
We will do what is right.

We will follow God.

We will tell the truth,
We will not tell lies.

We will follow God.

We will be good to our brother,
We will not hurt our neighbour.

We will follow God.

The second thing Jesus teaches us is this: we must share the love of God with everybody else.

The Reading comes from the Gospel of Saint John.

One day Jesus said to his followers:

'I love you all very much.
I want you to be happy like me,
so I will tell you what you must do.
Love everyone else
in the same way as I have loved you.

'If you do,
I will call you my friends.'

If we listen to Jesus and get on with what he tells us to do, we will be as 'safe as houses'.

The Reading comes from the Gospel of Saint Matthew.

One day Jesus said:

'It's no good just saying
that you will do what my Father wants!
You must really get on with it!

'But if you do as I tell you,
you will be as safe as the man
who built his house on a rock.
    The rains came and the land became flooded.
    The wind blew and lashed against the house.
    But it did not fall down,
    because it was built firmly on a rock.

'But if you don't do as I tell you,
you won't be safe at all!
You will be like the man who built his house on sand,
    and when the rain fell and the wind blew
    the house fell down,
    because it was only built on sand!'

Jesus tells us what God the Father wants us to do.

Here are some of the things that God wants us to do and some of the things he does not *want us to do.*

The Reading comes from the Book of Moses.

God says:

You must not tell lies about other people.
You must not hate anyone.

If someone has done wrong,
tell them they have done wrong,
but don't try to get your own back.
Don't grumble either!

You must take care of each other
just as much as you take care of yourself.

47  'YOU ARE MY FRIENDS'

God our Father still loves us in spite of all the things we do wrong.

The Reading comes from one of the Letters of Saint Paul.

Dear Titus,

When we were baptised,
we all became the children of God.

This proves how good and kind God is
because he still loved us
even though we did not deserve it!

When we were baptised,
he gave us the Spirit of his Love
to help us to be kind and loving like himself.

He did all this
because he wanted us to be his children
and to be happy with him for ever.

Jesus says: 'I don't want you just to work for me, I want you to be my friends.'

The Reading comes from the Gospel of Saint John.

One day Jesus said:

'I don't want you just to work for me
and do as you're told.

'I want you to be my friends
and be happy with me.

'But remember,
you did not choose me,
I chose you to be my friends,
and I want you to be friends with each other.'

This is one of the most famous of all the stories of Jesus and it reminds us that God our Father is always ready to forgive us if we are sorry.

The Reading comes from the Gospel of Saint Luke.

One day Jesus told his friends this story.

There was once a farmer
who had two sons.
The younger son came to his Father and said:
'Isn't it about time
that you gave me my share of the farm?'
So the Father gave him his share of the money.

A few days later,
the boy packed his bags and left home.
He went a long way away
and he had a good time,
but he wasted all his money,
until at last he didn't even have enough
to buy something to eat.
So he had to get a job on a farm
feeding the pigs,
and he was so hungry,
he would even have eaten the pig-swill
if he could have got it!

Then he began to think.
'What a fool I am!' he said to himself.
'Even the men who only *work* for my Father
have as much as they want to eat!
And here am I, starving to death!
I know I have hurt God
and I've hurt my Father,
but I'm going back home!
I'll tell my Father I am sorry,
and I'll ask him to give me a job as a workman
   because I'm not good enough to be called his son any more.'

So he went home again,
and his Father saw him coming.
He felt sorry for the boy,
and ran out to meet him
   and made him welcome.
The boy began to say, 'I have done wrong . . .'
But his Father did not wait for him to finish.
He told his servants to get out some good clothes for the boy
and to get a meal ready.

'I thought I had lost my boy,' he said,
'I thought he was dead!
But now he is alive again,
and I have found him once more!'

The other son was out working in the fields,
but when he came back to the house,
he heard the sound of music and dancing.
'What's going on?' he asked.
'Your brother has come back home,' said one of the workmen,
'and your Father's so pleased to have him home safely
that he's decided to have a party for him!'
The older boy was furious when he heard this.
He was so angry he wouldn't even come into the house.
So his Father came outside to him and said,
'Come on in and enjoy yourself.'
'No, I won't,' said the boy,
'this son of yours has wasted everything.
Why have you put on a feast like this for *him*?
I've worked for you like a slave for years
and you've never let me have even a *little* party with *my* friends.'

'My son,' said the Father,
'you were always safe at home with me,
and everything I had was yours as well as mine.
But your brother, he was dead – and now he is alive!
We've got to be happy – we've got to have a feast,
for I had lost him, and now I have found him again!'

*God our Father has forgiven us, now we should try and forgive other
people when they do wrong to us.*
The Reading comes from one of the Letters of Saint Paul.

Dear Friends,

God loves you,
so you must be kind to each other.

Be patient
and put up with each other.

Be ready to forgive,
as soon as an argument begins,
because God has forgiven you.

49 ✠ 'TEACH US TO PRAY!'

Jesus prays to his Father – so should we!
The Reading comes from the Gospel of Saint Luke.

One day Jesus was saying his prayers
and when he had finished,
one of his friends said,
'Teach us to pray!'
So Jesus told them to say this prayer:

'Father,
we want everyone to praise you,
and we want your kingdom to grow better and better
   until it is perfect.

'Give us enough food each day,
forgive us when we do wrong,
   just as we forgive others
   when they do wrong to us,
and help us when we are put to the test.'

✠

The Holy Spirit will help us to pray, if we don't know what to say.
The Reading comes from one of the Letters of Saint Paul.

Dear Friends,

Sometimes we find it hard to say our prayers!
But remember we have a special friend –
the Holy Spirit!
and he will help us.

Sometimes we don't know what to say to God,
but the Holy Spirit will help us
to pray without using words,
and God will understand.

There are a lot of things we should do, but one thing is more important than nearly all the others, and that is – we must say 'thank you' to God.

The Reading comes from one of the Letters of Saint Paul.

Dear Friends,

Help your teachers,
and don't make life difficult for them.
Don't fight each other,
don't be lazy,
and help the people who are nervous.

Take care of the children who are not very well.
Be patient.
Don't try to get your own back
and think of what would be best for everyone.

But most important of all,
  be happy
  and say 'thank you' to God
  for all the good things he gives to you.

⊠

This is the story of the man who said 'thank you' to Jesus.
The Reading comes from the Gospel of Saint Luke.

One day Jesus went up to Jerusalem
and while he was on his way,
he went into a little town nearby.

Ten lepers came out to meet him there,
and they waved across to him, saying,
'Please help us, Jesus!'

When he saw them, Jesus said,
'Go and see the priest!'
So they did,
and as they were on their way,
they were healed!

One of the ten came straight back to Jesus
and he praised God at the top of his voice,
throwing himself down in front of Jesus.
'Thank you, Jesus,' he said,
'Thank you very much!'

Jesus then said,
'Didn't all the others get better as well?
Or have they just not bothered
to come and say thank you?
I wonder why you are the only one who came back.
Stand up my friend,' he said,
'God loves you for what you have done.'

51 ✠ 'WORKING FOR JESUS'

Jesus does the job that God the Father has given him to do!

The Reading comes from the Gospel of Saint John.

One day Jesus said,

'My Father is always hard at work,
   and so am I!'

This made a lot of people angry,
because Jesus said that God was his own father
and they didn't like that.

So Jesus said,
'I am not doing anything by myself,
I am only doing what I can see my Father is doing.
I am doing as I am told
   – not just doing what I want to do myself.
Surely this will prove to you
   that I have come from my Father in heaven.'

✠

God our Father gives all of us a job to do as well.

The Reading comes from one of the Letters of Saint Paul.

Dear Friends,

God is making things better all the time.
He knows all the people who love him
and he gives them each a job to do
so they can work with him.

He wants us all to become more like his Son, Jesus,
for Jesus is our eldest brother
in the family of God.

It would be a pity if we didn't enjoy ourselves. The followers of Jesus shouldn't be glum, we should be happy people.

The Reading comes from the Book of the Preacher.

It is wonderful to see the brightness of the sunshine.
It is good to enjoy ourselves all through our lives,
   and especially when we are young.

There's so much to do!
There's so much to see!

May you always be healthy.
May you never be sad!

This is one of the most beautiful stories about Jesus. Everyone seems to be happy, as if they were all enjoying a holiday!

The Reading comes from the Gospel of Saint John.

One night some of the friends of Jesus
happened to meet each other.
There were Peter and Thomas
and James and John and three others.

Simon Peter said,
'I'm going fishing!'
and the others all said,
'We'll come as well!'

So the whole lot of them got into Peter's boat
and began to put out the nets.
But they didn't catch anything all night.
In the morning
just as it was getting light, ·
they saw Jesus on the shore.

He shouted over to them and said,
'Have you caught anything, my friends?'
and they said 'No!'

Then Jesus said,
'Throw your net over the other side of the boat
and you'll find something there.'

So they did,
and they caught so many fish
they could hardly pull in the net!

When they came back to land,
they found that Jesus had already made a little fire
and was cooking some fish.
He also had some bread as well.

'Bring over some of your fish,'
he said to Peter,
'and come and have some breakfast.'

53 ✠ THE NEW RULE

Jesus gives his followers a new rule: they must live like him.
The Reading comes from the Gospel of Saint John.

One day Jesus said:

Take care of each other.
This is my new rule: *Love each other*
just as much as I have loved you.

If you do,
people will notice
and they will say – 'You are like Jesus.'

✠

If we are really good, we will not have to 'pretend' to be good.
The Reading comes from one of the Letters of Saint Paul.

Dear Friends,

Don't just pretend to be good,
really try to be kind
and try not to be bad.

You are part of God's family
and you must take care of each other
like good brothers and sisters.

Don't forget to share your things with each other.
And when you have to work,
don't be lazy!
Do it for the sake of Jesus.
Trust God and he will make you happy.
Don't give up
if things are difficult.

And, of course, always remember to say your prayers.

God knows everything about us, He knows what we can *do and what we cannot do. So he really knows when we are doing our best!*

The Reading comes from the Book of Praise.

You know me, Lord, so very well,
you know when I get up,
you know when I go back to sleep.
You know each thing I do.

You know what I am going to say
    before I even talk!
You are always close to me.
You're wonderful, O God.

So if I climb the highest hill,
you would be there with me.
And if I swam beneath the waves,
you'd still be there with me!

Even in the dark at night,
you would be next to me.
Yes, even then, I could not hide,
you would be there with me.

Here is one of the stories of Jesus. It tells about some people who were given a lot of money. Some of them made good use of it, but one man did not – and that was a pity because he could have done if he had only tried.

The Reading comes from the Gospel of Saint Luke.

One day Jesus told this story to his friends.

Once upon a time there was a king
who had to go on a journey to a country far away.
So he called for all his servants before he left,
and gave each of them a gold coin.
'Here is some money,' he said,
'I want you all to make good use of it while I am away.'

When he came back,
the King asked all his servants to come and see him again.

The first man came forward and said,
'Lord, you gave me one gold coin.
See how well I have used it.
Look! Now I have ten gold coins!'

'That's good,' said the King,
'You *have* made good use of my money.
I will put you in charge of ten cities!'

Then the second man came forward and said,
'Lord, you gave me one gold coin.
Look! Now I have made five gold coins!'

Very good,' said the King,
'I will put you in charge of five of my cities.'

But one man came forward and said,
'Lord, here is your gold coin.
I hid it away in a handkerchief,
and I didn't do anything with it,
because I was afraid of what you might say.'

And the King was very angry when he heard this,
because the man had not made any use of his gold coin at all.

55   'FORGIVE YOUR BROTHER!'

If we forgive other people, then God will forgive us when we do wrong.

The Reading comes from the Book of a Wise Man called Ben Sirah.

If a man is angry with someone else,
how can he expect God to be gentle with him.

If a man is unkind to a person like himself,
how can he dare to ask God to be kind to him.

If a man will not forgive others
how can he expect anyone to forgive him.

This is one of the stories of Jesus. It tells the story of a man who didn't know how to forgive.

The Reading comes from the Gospel of Saint Matthew.

One day Jesus told his friends this story.

There was once a King
who decided to sort out all his money,
and he discovered that one of his servants
owed him a thousand pounds!
The servant couldn't pay any of it back,
so the King said that he would have to go to prison!

The servant threw himself down in front of the King
and he said,
'Give me some more time,
and I will pay it all back.'
This made the King feel so sorry for him,
that he let his servant go free
    and he didn't ask him to pay back anything at all!

Now just as this servant left the King's Palace,
he happened to meet another of the King's servants,
and he remembered that *he* owed him five pounds!
So he grabbed him by the throat,
nearly choking him to death
and said,
'You owe me some money.
Give me it all back at once!'

'I cannot,' the man replied,
'but I will, if you give me some more time to pay!'
'Oh no!' said the servant,
'If you cannot pay everything now,
you will have to go to prison!'

Everyone was very upset
when they heard what had happened,
and they told the King about it.

So the King sent for the servant and said,
'What a wicked servant you are!
You asked me to be kind to you
and I was – very kind!
But you wouldn't be even a little bit kind to someone else!
You can go straight to prison,
and you will stay there
until you pay every penny you owe me!'

Then Jesus said,
'You must learn to forgive each other,
or my Father will treat you as you treat others.'

56 THE KINDNESS OF A STRANGER

We must love God and we must love our neighbour.

The Reading comes from the Gospel of Saint Luke.

One day a man came to Jesus and said,
'What do you think I should do,
if I want to please God?'

Jesus said,
'What does the Bible say about this?'

And the man said,
'You must love God
with all your heart,
with all your strength
and with all your mind,

and you must love your neighbour
as much as you love yourself.'

Jesus then said,
'You are right!
If you do this,
you will really please God,
and you will be really alive!'

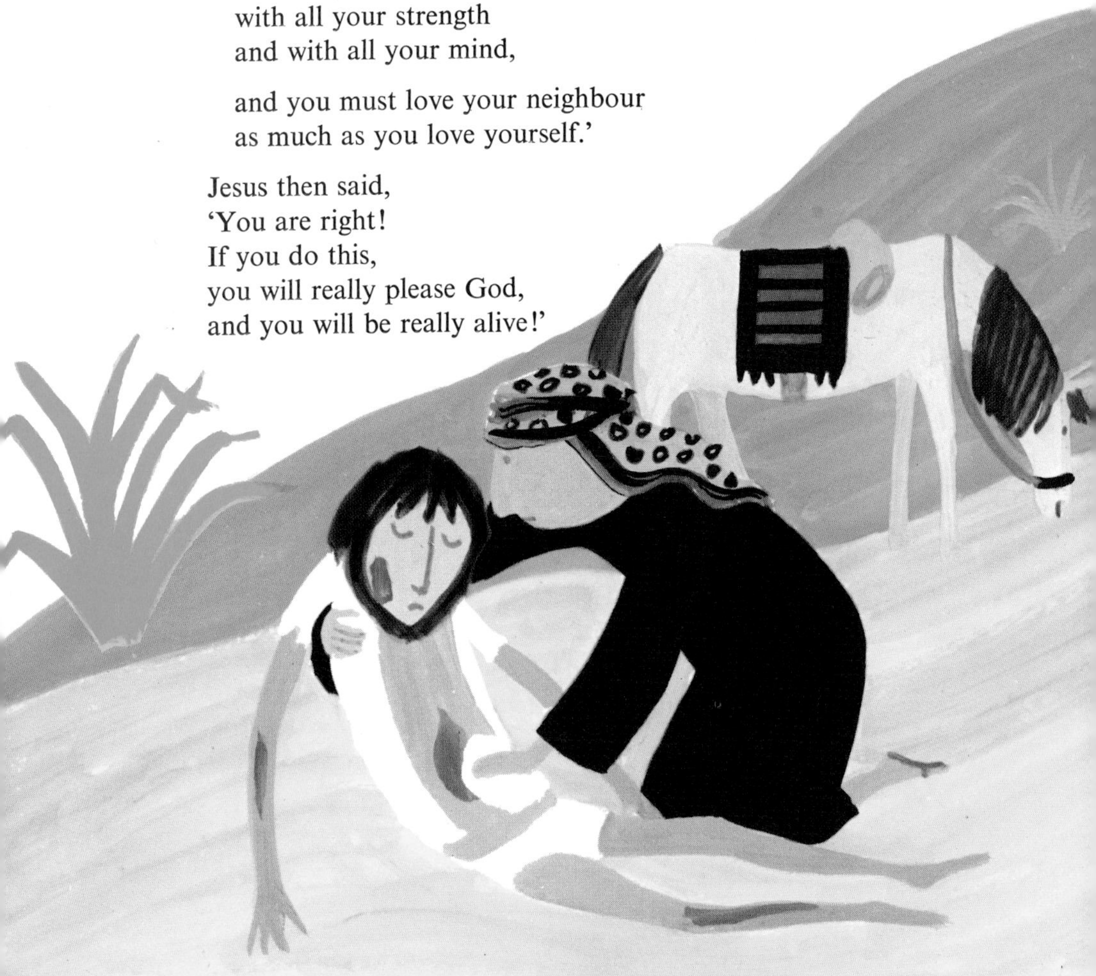

This is one of the greatest stories of Jesus. No one expects a stranger to stop and help the man who is beaten up, but in this story he does.

The Reading comes from the Gospel of Saint Luke.

One day, Jesus told this story:

There was once a man
who was going from Jerusalem to Jericho,
and he was attacked by bandits.
They tore off his clothes
and beat him up,
leaving him half dead on the road.

A few minutes later,
a Priest went down the same road.
But he didn't stop to help the poor man,
he went straight past
on the other side of the road.

Then a Teacher came along as well,
but he hurried past in the same way.

Then a stranger came.
He felt sorry for the poor man,
so he went across to him.
He bandaged up his wounds,
then he put him over his horse,
and took him to a hotel,
and looked after him all night.

Next morning he had to go away again,
so he left enough money
for the man to stay a bit longer in the hotel,
and he promised to come back later
and pay his bill.

Then Jesus said,
'That's what I call a real friend!'

57 ☒ THE POOR OLD WOMAN

Money is very useful – but it isn't everything!
The Reading comes from one of the Letters of Saint Paul.

Dear Timothy,

Tell people to be happy with what they have.

Remember that when we were born,
  we had nothing at all!
And when we die,
  we take nothing with us!

As long as we have enough to eat,
and enough to wear,
we should be satisfied.
If we worry about money all the time,
we may start to forget about God!

☒

This is the story of the old woman who was still very generous to other
people even though she was very poor herself.

The Reading comes from the Gospel of Saint Mark.

One day Jesus went into the Temple
and while he was there,
he saw all the people putting their money
into the 'Poor Box'.

Some of the rich people put in a lot of money,
but then a poor old woman came along
and put in two little coins worth a penny!

Jesus saw this happen,
and he said to his friends,
'That woman has put in more money than all the rest.
For they put in the money they had to spare,
but she has put in *everything* she has.'

God says 'Don't forget about the poor.'
The Reading comes from the Book of a Wise Man called Isaiah.

God says:
Remember,
it is no good saying your prayers to me,
if you go on hurting each other,
or if you keep on arguing and fighting,
and punching each other.

You must share things.
You must feed the hungry,
and get houses for the poor people,
and buy clothes for the people who haven't got enough.

If you do this,
you will make the whole world bright,
you will be like the sun
that fills the sky with light each morning.

⊠

God does not forget the poor. He will take care of those who cannot help themselves. This poem is from the Book of Praise.

God will remember the poor,
when they cry.
He will never forget them.
He will take care of the weak and the helpless.

He is kind and he is loving.
He will not forget them
when they are in danger.
He will not leave them
to die of starvation,
for he loves them too much.

This is one of the stories of Jesus. It tells the story of two men. One of them was very rich, and the other was very poor.

The Reading comes from the Gospel of Saint Luke.

One day Jesus told his friends this story.

There was once a very rich man,
who used to wear lots of expensive clothes,
and eat lots of food each day.

But outside his house
lay a very poor man called Lazarus,
who was very hungry,
and his body was covered in sores.

One day the poor man died
and went straight to heaven.
The rich man died as well,
but he went straight to hell.

Then the rich man looked up
and he saw Lazarus a long way away in heaven
and he said,
'Come and help me!
Dip the tip of your finger in water,
and come and put it on my tongue,
for I am so hot and thirsty!'

But God said,
'You had a good time when you were alive,
Lazarus had a bad time.
Now you have changed places!
and you are having to suffer
while he is enjoying himself!'

If we really try to help other people, that is as good as helping Jesus himself.

The Reading comes from the Gospel of Saint Matthew.

One day Jesus was talking to his friends
and he said:

One of these days I will say,
'When I was hungry, you gave me something to eat.
When I was thirsty, you gave me something to drink.
When I was a stranger, you made me feel at home.
When I was cold, you gave me something warm to wear.
When I was ill, you came to see me.'

Then you will say,
'When were *you* hungry,
and when did *we* give you something to eat?
When were you thirsty,
when did we give you something to drink?
When were you a stranger,
when did we make you feel at home?
When were you cold,
when did we give you something warm to wear?
When were you ill,
when did we come to see you?'

Then I will say,
'If you tried to help anyone at all,
you did something for me!'

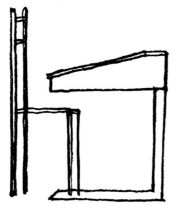

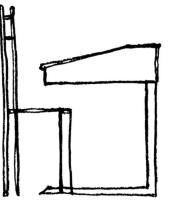

We all have a different job to do in the 'Body of Jesus'.
The Reading comes from one of the Letters of Saint Paul.

Dear Friends,

Look at yourselves.
Can you see how you have a body
with lots of different parts!

Each part has a special job to do, hasn't it?
If we are working with Jesus,
then we are all like the parts of one body,
for we are all joined together
and we all have a special job to do.

One job is to try and help other people,
and if that is our job
we should do it cheerfully.

Another job is to give up our money
to help people who haven't got any.
If that is our job,
we should be generous.

Yet another job is to be put in charge of something.
If that is our job,
we should do it carefully and well.

If we all do our own jobs,
then we will make the body of Jesus work properly.

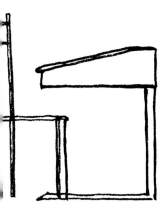

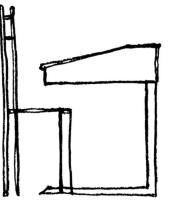

60  'STOP ARGUING!'

Don't cause trouble for others!

The Reading comes from the Book of a Wise Man called Isaiah.

Don't make trouble for other people.
Don't wave your fists about in the air,
and don't shout at people!

God will show you how to live
and he will make you strong.

Remember,
God will always listen to you,
and if you call for help,
he will say, 'I am with you!'

Even the friends of Jesus
sometimes had an argument
with each other. But Jesus soon settled them.

The Reading comes from the Gospel of Saint Mark.

One day
Jesus had been out with some of his friends,
and when they came back home, he said,
'What were you arguing about
on the road back there?'

When he asked them this,
they were very quiet,
because they had been fighting about
who was the greatest among them.

So Jesus sat down and said,
'If any of *you* want to be really big,
you will have to take care of everyone else!
Only the person who looks after other people first
will be great
while I'm around!'

61 'DON'T BE SAD'

When we die, we go to live with our Father in heaven.
The Reading comes from one of the Letters of Saint Paul.

Dear Friends,

I want to tell you something about people who die,
because I don't want you to be terribly sad
   like other people are,
for we are Christians!
We know that Jesus died just as we do,
but then he went to live with his Father in heaven.

We will do the same.
We will go to live with God our Father for ever.

I am certain of this,
because Jesus said it was true.

If someone dies, we must try not to get too upset.
Don't forget that God knows what is happening,
and he will take care of everything.

The Reading comes from the Gospel of Saint John.

One day Jesus said to his friends,

'Don't get upset,
trust God the Father
and trust me.

'There is plenty of room in my Father's house,
and I am going to get a place ready
   for each one of you.

'Then I will come back
and take you with me,
and you will be able to stay with me for ever.'

62 ⊠ ABRAHAM TRUSTED GOD

Abraham trusted God and he believed what God told him,
for he knew that God would not let him down.

The Reading comes from the Book of Beginnings.

God told Abraham that he would be famous.
He promised to look after Abraham's family,
and he said he would give them somewhere to live.

But Abraham lived in a tent,
and wandered around the desert with his sheep,
and he didn't even have any children.

One night Abraham was standing outside his tent,
looking up at the stars,
and he wondered how many stars there were.
He couldn't even begin to count them all!
Then God told him,
'You will have as many children as there are stars!'
And Abraham believed what God said.
Then he fell asleep
and dreamed that God came to him
like a great fire that burned in the dark!
And God said,
'I promise you, I will be your friend.'

✛

This poem was written by a man like Abraham who knew he could trust God all the time. It comes from the Book of Praise.

Blessed be God!

He listens to me,
he hears me when I pray for help.
Blessed be God!

I trust the Lord
for he is strong.
Blessed be God!

I thank the Lord
for he takes care of me.
Blessed be God!

✛

Jesus reminds us that Abraham trusted God and believed in him.

The Reading comes from the Gospel of Saint John.

One day, Jesus was talking to some people
who were angry with him.

They said,
'We don't believe what *your* Father says,
we only believe what Abraham has told us.
Abraham is our "Father",
and we don't want to know anything about *your* Father!'

But Jesus replied,
'If you were really children of Abraham,
you would believe in my Father
just as Abraham himself did!
And you wouldn't want to kill me
just because I have told you what my Father has said.
Abraham would never have done that!'

Moses was nearly drowned when he was a little baby. But God took extra special care of him because he wanted Moses to be the leader of his People when he grew up.

The Reading comes from the Book of Moses.

A long time ago
a man became King in Egypt
who hated the Jews,
because there were so many of them.
So he decided
to have all the Jewish baby boys drowned!

One day a Jewish baby was born
and his mother thought he was so beautiful
that she hid him away and kept him alive.
But in the end he became too big to hide,
and she had to find a way to get rid of him safely.
So she got a basket and painted it with tar
to keep out the water,
and she put her baby in the basket
and left the basket floating in the river.
But she told her daughter
to keep watching it
to see what happened to him.

A Princess came down to the river to have a swim,
and one of her servants saw the basket
as she walked along the riverside.
'Pull it out!' said the Princess,
so the servant did
and the Princess felt so sorry for the baby
she decided to keep him.

Just then the baby's sister came along and said,
'Shall I find someone to look after the baby for you?'
and the Princess said 'Yes.'

So the little girl went to get her own mother,
and then the Princess *paid* the woman
to look after *her own* baby!
But when the baby grew up,
the Princess made him just like her own son
and called him Moses.

Jesus was nearly killed when he was a baby – just like Moses! But God the Father did not want him to die so soon and took good care of him, so Jesus escaped.

The Reading comes from the Gospel of Saint Matthew.

Soon after Jesus was born,
Joseph was told that King Herod was looking for the child
and wanted to kill him!

Some Wise Men had come to King Herod
and told him that a new king called Jesus
was going to be born in Bethlehem.
They had promised to come back again
when they found him
and tell King Herod where he was,
but then they didn't come back at all,
and the King was furious!
So he murdered *all* the little baby boys in Bethlehem!

But Joseph escaped into Egypt with Jesus and his mother.

64   SAMUEL: THE BOY WHO LISTENED TO GOD

This is the story of Samuel, the boy who heard the voice of God.
The Reading comes from the Story of the Kings.

A long, long time ago,
there was a priest called Eli.
He was very old and was going blind.
But a young boy, called Samuel, looked after him.

One night, while Samuel was in bed,
he heard someone calling his name,
'Samuel! Samuel!'
So he got up and went to Eli and said,
'Here I am, what do you want?'
But Eli said,
'*I* didn't call you!
Go back to bed.'
So Samuel went and lay down again.

But it happened once more,
and Samuel went back to Eli,
and again Eli told him to go back to bed!

But when it happened a third time,
Eli said,
'Next time you must say,
"Yes, Lord, I'm listening." '

And it did happen again,
for God came and stood beside Samuel
and called his name,
and Samuel said,
'Yes, Lord, I'm listening.'
And then God spoke to Samuel,
and told him what he was going to do.

After that God was always very close to Samuel
and when the boy grew up,
he always listened to what God told him.

We talk to God in our prayers and then he is very close to us as well.

The Reading comes from the Gospel of Saint Matthew.

One day Jesus said,
'When you say your prayers,
don't worry so much about the things you want,
remember that you have a Father in Heaven
who knows all about the things you need.

'When *you* say your prayers,
promise him to try and do what he wants,
and he will give you everything you need as well!'

65 ⊠ DAVID: THE BOY WHO LOOKED AFTER THE SHEEP

This is the story of a boy called David who was very close to God.
The Reading comes from the Book of Samuel.

A long, long time ago there was a man called Samuel.

One day God told Samuel to go and choose someone
to be the new king.
God said,
'I want you to find a new king for me.
I don't mind what he looks like!
He doesn't have to be tall and handsome!
Some people only think a man is good if he *looks* good,
but I can see how good a man really is!'

Samuel went to Bethlehem
to the house of a man called Jesse,
and he looked at the seven sons of Jesse one by one.
But he knew God did not want any of these!

So he said,
'Have you any more children?'
'Yes,' said Jesse,
'you haven't seen my youngest boy yet,
but he's out, looking after the sheep.'
'Bring him here,' said Samuel,
and Jesse brought in David.

David was a good-looking boy
with red cheeks and bright eyes,
and Samuel knew at once that *he* was the right person!

So he blessed David
and poured oil on his head
(to show that God was going to make him strong and good).
And from then on
God was always very close to the boy.

130

Jesus prays that God may be close to all of us, then we will know that he loves us.

The Reading comes from the Gospel of Saint John.

Just before he died,
Jesus said this prayer to his Father in heaven.

'Father, keep my friends safe!
May you be as close to them
    as you are close to me.
And may they be happy
    and free from all harm!'

66 ✠ DAVID AND GOLIATH

This is the story of how David killed Goliath, even though David was only a little boy and Goliath was a big strong man.
The Reading comes from the Book of Samuel.

A long, long time ago there was a boy called David,
who lived with his seven brothers in Bethlehem.
His three eldest brothers were soldiers,
and one day their father sent David
to the camp where all the soldiers lived
to take some bread and cheese to his brothers.

David got up early that morning
and asked someone else to look after his sheep for him,
then he set off for the camp.

When he got there,
the soldiers were getting ready to start fighting,
so David left his bag
    with the man who looked after the luggage,
and went to see his brothers as quickly as he could.
While he was talking to them,
Goliath, the best soldier in the enemy army, came along
and said he would fight anyone who thought they could beat him.
But everyone ran away
because they were all afraid of him.

So David said,
'What will you give me if I kill him?'
But his brothers said,
'No, you can't!
Go away, go home!
What are you doing here anyway?
Who is looking after your sheep?
You've just come here for the fun of it
    to see the fighting.'

King Saul heard what David had said
and sent for him.
'You can't go and fight Goliath,' said King Saul.
'You're only a little boy,
and he's a big tall man!'
But David said,
'Oh yes I can!
I have killed a lion and a bear before now
    when they attacked my sheep,
so I can easily kill Goliath!'

So the King said,
'Well, you can always have a go.
May God help you.
You can use my breast plate and my helmet,
and you can take my big sword with you as well.'
But David said,
'I couldn't even walk with all those on,
I'm not used to wearing them!

All I want is my stick and my sling
and five smooth pebbles from the river.'

When little David came out with his sling,
Goliath just laughed at him.
But David said,
'Don't laugh! You think you are strong
   because you have a sword and a spear,
but I have God to help me
   and he is much stronger than you are!'
Then he put a stone in his sling,
swung it round and round,
and let it go,
and the stone flew straight towards Goliath
and hit him on the forehead and killed him!

Then all the enemy soldiers ran away
when they saw their best soldier had been killed!

*David was obviously very brave. In this reading Jesus tells us that we must
be brave as well.*

The Reading comes from the Gospel of Saint Luke.

Jesus spent the last few days of his life in Jerusalem,
and each day he went to the Temple to teach the people
– this is what he said to them:

'Keep praying that you will be brave,
pray that you will keep going
and then you won't let me down!'

Lots of people used to come to the Temple each morning
   just to hear Jesus,
and he stayed there all day long speaking to them.
Then in the evening
Jesus would go out to the Olive Hill near Jerusalem
   to pray during the night.

David and Jonathan were the best of friends. They knew they could trust each other and they knew they would never let each other down.

The Reading comes from the Story of Samuel.

A long time ago there was a king called Saul,
who became very unhappy with himself,
   though he didn't know why.
One day he said to his soldiers,
'Find me a man who can play the harp really well,
and bring him to me
so that he can play for me and cheer me up.'
One of his soldiers said,
'I have seen David, the son of Jesse, playing the harp,
and he plays very well indeed.
He's also a brave fighter and very sensible.'

So King Saul sent for David,
and when he came,
the King asked him to stay with him.
Whenever the King felt upset and miserable,
David used to play his harp
and the King would listen.
Then he would feel much better again.
King Saul thought David was wonderful.

The King had a son called Jonathan,
and Jonathan became David's friend.
In fact they became such good friends
that one day Jonathan gave David his cloak and his belt
   and his sword and bow as well,
and they promised to be friends for ever.

Everyone liked David
for he was such a good fighter.

But then King Saul began to get jealous of him,
and one day, when the King was feeling upset and miserable,
he said to Jonathan,
'I am going to kill David!'

So Jonathan went out to his friend and said,
'My father wants to kill you,
so you must go and hide in the fields,
until I find out what's wrong,
then I'll come and let you know.'

Next morning, Jonathan went back to his father and said,
'Please don't hurt David.
He's done nothing wrong to you.
He has done everything possible to help you.'
In the end he made his father agree with him,
and King Saul said,
'I promise God
I will not hurt your friend.'
So Jonathan went to David
and told him everything that had happened,
and he brought David back to live with the King again.

It's good to have friends, especially when we know they will not let us down. Jesus liked his friends just as we do, and he liked to be together with them, as all friends do.

The Reading comes from the Gospel of Saint Mark.

Jesus went round all the villages near Nazareth
and he told everyone the 'Good News from God'.
Then he called 'the Twelve' together
and sent them out in twos
so that they could go and do the same as him.

When they came back,
they wanted to tell Jesus
about all the things they had said
and everything they had done.
So Jesus said,
'You haven't even had time for anything to eat.
Let's go away to a quiet place
by ourselves,
and have a rest.'

So they did,
and they all went off to a quiet place
where they could be by themselves.

John the Baptist said – 'Get ready for God!' So did Isaiah.

The Reading comes from the Book of a Wise Man called Isaiah.

A long, long time ago, Isaiah said,

Can you hear the voice of God?
Listen to what he is saying.

'Make a straight road for him to walk along.
Fill in the valleys,
and flatten the hills.'

Then you will see God.
Everyone will see him,
for God has said so himself!

⊠

Except for Jesus himself, there never was anyone greater than John the Baptist!

The Reading comes from the Gospel of Saint Matthew.

John the Baptist lived down by the River Jordan.
He didn't wear expensive clothes,
and he didn't eat very much,
but lots of people came to see him.

He used to say,
'Stop doing wrong,
God is going to send you a King.'

Then everyone would tell God they were sorry
for doing wrong,
and John would pour water over them in the river,
(and make them clean).

This is the story of how Mary went to look after Elizabeth while Elizabeth was having a baby.

The Reading comes from the Gospel of Saint Luke.

One day, Mary heard
that her cousin, Elizabeth, was going to have a baby.

So she went as quickly as she could
into the hills to the town where Elizabeth lived.

Mary went into Elizabeth's house
and said 'Hello, how are you?'
And Elizabeth replied,
'I am proud
that you have come to visit me,
because the Lord has given you
a special blessing!
He has given you a special child!'

Then Mary said,
'I praise the Lord for he is good.
He makes me glad!
I am young and I am poor,
and yet he comes and chooses me!
And from now on,
everyone will say that he has blessed me.

'The Lord is strong, the Lord is generous,
stretching out his hand to help the sick,
feeding hungry people with good food,
looking after people everywhere!

'Long ago he said that he would help us.
Now the Lord
    has kept his promise perfectly!
He has not forgotten his own people.
He has come to rescue them
and keep them safe!'

Jesus said 'If you want to be like my mother, you must do what God the Father wants.'

The Reading comes from the Gospel of Saint Mark.

One day Jesus went home
and so many people came to see him
and he was so busy
that he didn't even have time to eat anything.

When his family heard about this
they said he was mad,
and they came along to help him.
But there were so many people outside the house
they couldn't even get anywhere near him.
So they sent him a message, saying,
'Your mother and the rèst of your family
    are outside
and they want to see you.'

Inside the house
everyone was sitting round Jesus in a circle,
and he looked round at them all and said,
'You will all be my brothers and my sisters
and my mother as well,
if you do what God wants you to do.'

When almost everyone else had run away Mary stood by the cross near her Son. At least she didn't let him down.

The Reading comes from the Gospel of Saint John.

When Jesus was on the cross,
his mother stood beside him,
and her sister was there as well,
and Mary of Magdala.

Jesus looked at his mother,
and he looked at John, his best friend,
who was standing beside her,
and he said,
'Mother,
John will take care of you
    as if he was your own son.'
Then he said to John,
'I know she will be like a mother to you.'

And when Jesus had died,
John took Mary home
    to stay with him.

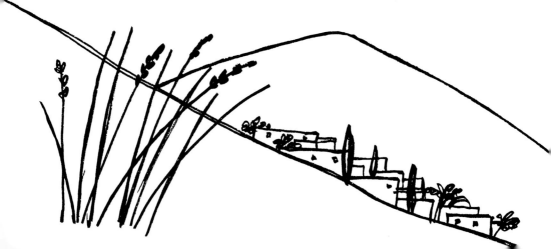

While the followers of Jesus were waiting for the Holy Spirit to come and tell them what to do, they spent most of their time praying together, and Mary was there to pray with them.

The Reading comes from the Story of the Apostles.

After the Ascension,
the friends of Jesus went back to the city,
and stayed in the room where they lived.

All the friends of Jesus were there,
Peter, John, James and Andrew,
Philip, Thomas and Bartholomew,
and Matthew, James, Simon and Jude.

And the women who were friends of Jesus
were there as well,
– and his mother, Mary.

And they spent their time together, praying.

71 ✠ THE FRIENDS OF JESUS STAY WITH HIM

*Even when the other people said they wouldn't follow Jesus, 'The Twelve'
did not let him down.*

The Reading comes from the Gospel of Saint John.

One day a lot of the friends of Jesus said,
'We don't like the things he tells us.
No one can believe *him*!'

Jesus heard them complaining and said,
'Why are you upset?'

But after that,
a lot of them left him,
and wouldn't follow him.

Then Jesus turned to 'The Twelve' and said,
'What about you?
Will you leave me as well?'

But Peter said,
'Who else could we go to?
You can tell us how to live,
and we believe what you tell us.'

✠

*We must try to follow Jesus like 'The Twelve', even if people try to put
us off.*
The Reading comes from one of the Letters of Saint Paul.

Dear Friends,

I can see God our Father loves you.
He has picked you out in a special way.

When I told you about Jesus,
it really made a difference to you
and you began to try and live like Jesus,
even though some people tried to put you off!

Do not tell lies about anyone!

The Reading comes from one of the Letters of Saint Paul.

Dear Titus,
Don't forget that we have all been silly sometimes,
and we have all done wrong ourselves.
There was a time
when we were horrible to people
and they didn't like us
because we were always doing wrong.

But then Jesus came to us
and showed us how to be kind.

So don't tell any more lies about people
and be friendly and polite to everyone.

✠

*No one would have thought that Saint Peter would tell a lie about Jesus,
and yet he did! But then he was very sorry for it and Jesus forgave him.*

The Reading comes from the Gospel of Saint Matthew.

When Jesus was arrested,
he was taken away to the Palace to be questioned.
So Peter followed him
    to see what was going to happen,
and he sat down in the courtyard outside the Palace
    and waited.

A servant girl came up to him and said,
'You were with Jesus of Galilee, weren't you?'
But he denied it in front of everyone and said,
'I don't know what you are talking about!'
Then he walked away
and stood near the gate.

Another servant girl saw him there
and she said to all the people,
'This man was with Jesus of Nazareth!'
Peter denied it again and said,
'By God, I do not know the man!'

A little later someone else came up and said,
'You are one of them, I know,
I can tell by the way you speak.'
Then Peter began to curse and swear,
'I tell you, I don't know him.'

Just then the cock crew
    and Peter suddenly remembered that Jesus had said:
'Peter, you will let me down in the morning!'
And when he thought of what he had just done,
    he went outside and began to cry
        for he was ashamed of himself.

God is always ready to forgive us.

The Reading comes from the Book of a Wise Man called Joel.

God says this –

Come back to me
    and be sorry.
Turn back to me,
    for I am gentle.

I am slow to lose my temper
and very quick to forgive you
    if you have done wrong.

✠

This is the story of Matthew, the Tax Man.

The Reading comes from the Gospel of Saint Matthew.

One day Jesus met a man called Matthew
who was a tax collector.
He was sitting in his house working
when Jesus came,
but Jesus said,
'Follow me!'
and Matthew got up at once
    and followed him.

Then he took Jesus for a meal
and he invited a lot of his old friends as well.
Some of the Teachers saw this and they said,
'Matthew's old friends are bad people!
Why does Jesus go and eat with *them*?'

But Jesus heard them saying this and said,
'I have come to *help* bad people, that's why.
I can't help the people who think they're all right!'

When we do wrong, we turn away from God. But God wants us to come back to him and he will help us to do so – like the shepherd who even carries back the sheep on his shoulders.

The Reading comes from the Gospel of Saint Luke.

One day Jesus said,

'If you had a hundred sheep,
and you lost one of them,
wouldn't you go and look for that one lost sheep
even if you had to leave all the others
   on the hillside by themselves?

'And when you found it again,
wouldn't you be happy
as you carried it home on your shoulders?
You would be so happy,
you would tell everyone else about it
   so that they could share your happiness.

'In the same way,
even if only one man has run away from God,
God will still be very happy
to welcome him back home.'

God is very happy to see anyone come back to him. But if we have done wrong by stealing, he would like us to give back what we have taken before we come and tell him we are sorry.

The Reading comes from the Gospel of Saint Luke.

One day, Jesus went to Jericho.

Now a man lived there called Zachaeus,
and he was very rich,
because he collected money for the Romans.

This man was very keen to see what Jesus looked like,
but he was only little,
and he couldn't see anything with all the people there.

So he ran on in front,
and climbed up a sycamore tree
just to see Jesus when he went past.
But Jesus saw him up the tree and said,
'Come down, I want to stay in your house today.'
So Zachaeus climbed down as quickly as he could,
and took him home.

Everyone else complained and said,
'He's a bad man,
Jesus shouldn't have gone there.'
But Zachaeus said,
'Look Jesus,
I'm going to give half of everything I've got to the poor!
And if I've cheated anyone,
I'll give him back four times as much as I took!'

75 ❧ THE SOLDIER WHO DID AS HE WAS TOLD

It's no good just saying you will do something, to keep people happy, if you are not really going to do it.

The Reading comes from the Gospel of Saint Matthew.

One day Jesus said,
I'm going to tell you a story,
and I want to know what you think about it.

There was a man who had two sons.
He went to one of the sons and said,
'Will you go and do a job for me today?'
but the lad said,
'No, I won't!'
Then later on he felt sorry
and he went and did the job!

The Father went to the other boy
and said the same thing
This boy said,
'Yes, certainly!'
But then he didn't go at all!

Then Jesus said,
'Which boy did what his Father wanted?'
And everyone said the same,
'It was the first boy
　　for he did the job in the end.'

This is the story of the Roman Soldier who was certain that Jesus could help his servant.

The Reading comes from the Gospel of Saint Luke.

There was once a Roman Soldier
and he had a servant who was ill and dying.
Now this servant was a very good servant,
so the Soldier sent some of his friends
to ask Jesus if he would come and help him.

When these friends came to Jesus, they said,
'This man has been very good to us.
He has even built our meeting house for us.'

So Jesus went along to the Soldier's house
and when he was nearly there,
the Soldier sent him another message, saying,
'Please don't let me trouble you!
I'm not good enough for you to come to me.
But if you just tell my servant to be better,
then I'm sure he will be all right again!
You see I know you can do this
because I am a soldier,
and *I* always do as I'm told.
I also expect everyone else to do the same!
If I say "Go!"
  then people go where I tell them.
If I say "Come here!"
  then they come to me.
If I say "Do that!"
  then they get on with it at once.'

When Jesus heard this, he was surprised
  and very pleased.
  'I haven't seen many people trust me like this,' he said.

  So he sent the messenger back to the Soldier
    and when they got back
    they found the servant was already better.

151

76 ⊞ THE MAN WHO CAME IN THROUGH THE ROOF

God is our Father and he can do anything!

The Reading comes from the Book of a Wise Man called Jeremiah.

God says,

Do not be afraid, my people,
for I will come and help you.

I hear that you are very ill!
No one can cure you,
no one can help you
and you cannot find a medicine
that will do you any good.

But I will make you healthy once more.
Yes I will make you better!

⊞

*Jesus is like God our Father, he can do anything! The man on the stretcher
obviously believed this!*

The Reading comes from the Gospel of Saint Mark.

When Jesus came back to Capernaum
the news got round that he was back
and so many people came to listen to him
they filled the house where he was,
and there wasn't even a space left in front of the door.

While Jesus was talking,
four men came with a man on a stretcher,
This man was paralysed and couldn't walk by himself,
and they wanted to bring him to Jesus.

There was no room for them to get in through the door.
So they made a hole in the roof
　　just over the place where Jesus was standing,
and lowered the stretcher down in front of him.

It was obvious they believed that Jesus could help the man.
Jesus could see that clearly,
so he said,
'Stand up, my friend.
Pick up your stretcher and go home.'
And the man *got* up,
　　and picked up his stretcher at once,
　　and walked out of the house all by himself!

Everyone was astonished when they saw this,
and they said:

'How good God is!'

We should never be spiteful.
The Reading comes from one of the Letters of Saint Paul.

Dear Friends,

From now on there's going to be no more telling lies.
You are going to tell the truth instead.

If you get angry with someone,
I want you to try and become friends again
  as soon as you can on the same day.

Don't lose your temper.
Don't shout at each other.
Don't call each other names,
and don't be spiteful!

Remember you have received
the gift of the Holy Spirit.
Therefore be friends with each other,
and forgive each other quickly,
because God has been quick to forgive you.

The bad thief was spiteful to Jesus, but the good thief became a saint!
The Reading comes from the Gospel of Saint Luke.

Jesus died on a cross,
at a place called the Hill of the Skull,
and two thieves were killed with him,
   one on either side.

There was a sign nailed to the cross of Jesus
and it said,
'This is the King of the Jews.'
So one of the thieves said,
'You're not much of a King, are you!'
But the other thief said,
'Don't say that!
He hasn't done anything wrong.'

Then he turned to Jesus and said,
'Don't forget me, will you?'

Jesus said,
'I promise you,
I will take you to heaven with me today!'

No one would have expected Saul to become a follower of Jesus. But strange things sometimes happen, and the greatest enemy of Jesus became his greatest friend.

The Reading comes from the Story of the Apostles.

A long time ago, there was a man called Saul,
and he hated the friends of Jesus so much
that he wanted to kill them all.
So he got permission to hunt them out
and put them in prison.

One day, he was riding on horse-back
to a city called Damascus,
and just as he came to the city walls,
he was thrown from his horse,
and saw a great flash of light.

Then he heard someone saying,
'Saul, Saul, why are you hurting me?'
'Who's that?' he said.
'I'm Jesus,' said the voice,
'and you're hurting *me*!'

Then Saul tried to get up,
but he couldn't see,
even with his eyes wide open.
Someone had to take his hand
and lead him into the city.

Jesus then sent a man called Ananias
to go and visit Saul.
Ananias didn't want to go
because he had heard all about this man
and he was afraid of him.
But God said he must go, so he did.

When Ananias found Saul,
he was saying his prayers
in a house in Straight Street.
So he went in and blessed him
with his hands outstretched over Saul.
'Brother Saul,' he said,
'Jesus has sent me to help you.
Receive the Holy Spirit.'
And at once Saul could see again,
    and he asked to be baptised immediately.

*Jesus wants everyone to come to him,
then they will get to know and love his Father
and receive the Holy Spirit.*

*The Reading comes from the Gospel of Saint
Matthew.*

Jesus said,

I want you to go everywhere
    and tell everyone what I have done.

Go and baptise them
    in the name of the Father
                and of the Son
                and of the Holy Spirit.

I have shown you how you should live,
now you must teach others to do the same.
I promise you
    I will always be near you to help you.

Jesus tells us that he always had to work very hard.
The Reading comes from the Gospel of Saint Luke.

One day Jesus was walking from one village to another
and a man came up to him and said,
'Jesus, I will follow you wherever you go!'

Jesus was pleased to hear him saying this
but he said to the man,
'You have to be ready to work hard,
    if you are going to follow me, you know.
Even a fox can go down a hole in the ground
    to have a rest,
and the birds can go back to their nests.
But I haven't even got a house to sleep in!'

It's hard work following in the footsteps of Jesus, as Saint Paul discovered for himself.

The Reading comes from one of the Letters of Saint Paul.

Dear Friends,

These are some of the things that have happened to me
while I have been telling people about Jesus.
I have had to work very hard.

I've been sent to prison.
I've been beaten up
   (in fact I was nearly killed once!)
I've been shipwrecked
   (and once I was lost out at sea all night!)

I've always been on the move
and I've often been afraid
   that I was going to be attacked by bandits.
I've had to get across rivers
   when there's been no bridge to walk over.

I've often had to go on working
without going to bed all night.

Sometimes I've been so hungry and thirsty
   that I've nearly died!

Once I even had some soldiers chasing me
and I had to get away by hiding in a basket
   and my friends lowered me out of their window
      over the city walls
   so that I could escape and go free.

Nevertheless I can put up with all this,
because I am doing it all for the sake of Jesus.

80 ✠ SAINT STEPHEN FORGAVE THE PEOPLE WHO KILLED HIM

We must always be ready to keep on forgiving people even if they do hurt us.

The Reading comes from the Gospel of Saint Luke.

One day Jesus said,

'If your friend does you wrong,
you can tell him off, if you like,
but if he says sorry,
  you must forgive him.
Even if he does wrong and upsets you
  seven times each day,
but then comes to you
  and says he is really sorry
you must keep on forgiving him.'

✠

Saint Stephen even forgave the people who were killing him.

The Reading comes from the Story of the Apostles.

One day, the twelve apostles
called a meeting of the friends of Jesus, and said:
We need someone to help us
to give out food
and look after people,
then *we* can teach and pray.

So they picked out Philip and Stephen and five others.
Then they prayed for them
and they blessed them,
  stretching their hands over them.

Stephen did wonderful things,
for he was very clever,
and the Holy Spirit helped him.
But some people told lies about him
    and had him arrested and put in prison.

The judge asked Stephen questions,
but no one would listen to his answers.
They put their hands over their ears,
    so they couldn't hear what he was saying.
Then they pulled him to a place outside the city
    and they threw stones at him
        until they killed him.

But before he died, Stephen said,
'Lord Jesus, I give you my life!
Do not blame them for doing wrong!'

81 ✠ SAINT PHILIP AND THE MAN IN A CHARIOT

Jesus and 'The Twelve' baptised many people.

The Reading comes from the Gospel of Saint John.

Jesus went with his friends into the countryside of Judea,
and he stayed there
   baptising many people
   – or at least his friends did.
They baptised even more people than John the Baptist.

But the Pharisees heard about it
   and they didn't like it.
So Jesus left Judea
and went back to Galilee.

✠

Saint Philip teaches a foreigner about Jesus and baptises him.

The Reading comes from the Story of the Apostles.

One of the followers of Jesus was called Philip.
One day Philip went out for a walk
along the desert road near Jerusalem.

As he was walking,
an important man went past in a chariot.
He was from Ethiopia
and was on his way home.

As he went along
he was reading the Bible
and Philip said,
'Do you understand what you are reading?'
'How can I by myself?' said the man,
'Come up here and sit beside me
   and explain it all.'

So Philip did,
and he went on to explain what Jesus had done.

After a while they came to some water,
and the man said,
'Is there any reason why I shouldn't be baptised here and now?'
and Philip said, 'No.'
So they stopped the chariot and got down,
and Philip baptised the man at once.

Jesus said, 'I want you to tell everyone what I have told you.'

The Reading comes from the Gospel of Saint Mark.

One day, Jesus said to his friends:

'Go out to the whole world.
Tell everyone what I have done
and baptise everyone who believes what you say.'

And they did just that:
after Jesus had died,
they talked about him everywhere.
And even though they could not see him,
Jesus helped them all the time.

⎋

Joseph Barnabas made the followers of Christ so well known that they were called 'Christ-ians' by everyone else.

The Reading comes from the Story of the Apostles.

One of the followers of Jesus
was a priest called Joseph Barnabas.
This man owned a field,
but he sold it
and gave the money he got for it to 'The Twelve'.

Later on
when Paul became a follower of Jesus
and everyone was afraid of him,
because they thought he was just pretending,
Joseph Barnabas took Paul to 'The Twelve'
and told them Paul's story,
so that people would trust Paul,
(even though he *had* been their enemy!)

Barnabas was a good man,
and the Holy Spirit filled him with the love of God.
So 'The Twelve' sent him to Antioch
   to help the followers of Jesus there.
And he taught a lot of people to know and love Jesus.

Then he went off to find Paul again,
and he brought Paul back to Antioch.
They stayed there together for twelve months,
teaching everyone about Jesus.
This made the followers of Jesus Christ so well known
that they were called 'the Christ-ians'
because they followed 'Christ'.

83 ✠ EVERYONE IS WELCOME IN THE PEOPLE OF GOD!

God the Father wants people to come and be happy with him. Some people don't seem to be interested – they just can't be bothered to follow his Son, Jesus. So God invites other people – in fact he invites everyone! He doesn't want anyone to be left out!

The Reading comes from the Gospel of St Luke.

One day Jesus told this story.

There was once a man who gave a great banquet
and invited many people to it.
When everything was ready,
he sent out his son to tell the guests
   to come and join him.
But each one of them began to make excuses.

One of the guests said,
'I've just bought a field,
and I have to go and look at it.
I'm sorry. I cannot come.'

Another guest said,
'I've just bought five pair of oxen,
and I've got to go and see what they're like.
I'm sorry. I cannot come.'
Yet another guest said,
'What a pity. I've just been married.
I'm sorry. I cannot come.'

When the man heard all this, he was furious,
and he said to his son,
'These people don't *deserve* to enjoy my banquet!
Go out into the streets and the alley-ways of the town,
and bring in the poor, the crippled, the blind and the lame.
Bring *them* into my banquet instead!'

When this was done, there was still some more room left,
and so the man said,
'Go right out into the country roads and lanes
and *make* people come in.
I don't want my house to be empty for the banquet!
I want it to be absolutely full!'

NOTE FOR PARENTS AND TEACHERS

This collection of readings had its beginning in a number of edited scriptural passages intended for use with young people. In these passages I tried to link together thematically the two readings that were usual in the liturgy of the Word, so as to give them a certain unity and to bring out their meaning. This small collection grew, and it was finally published as a volume of readings for young children under the title of *The Lord be With You*[1]. This present volume is directly based on the earlier collection.

My own method of editing and linking readings has undoubtedly developed considerably since I first began. Through working with much younger children I have become even more aware than before of the need to present each passage in a way that gives it a certain immediacy and directness. If this is not done, the scriptures can easily fail to reveal themselves in all their natural vividness and power. Sometimes the very depth of thought obscures the simple meaning of the scriptural author. A particular passage may deal with several distinct themes and ideas which need to be 'unravelled' if a young mind is to grasp them accurately. Although a reading may well be considering a subject that is extremely relevant to a child, this may be presented side by side with another more adult concern which is quite beyond him. The scriptures themselves developed into their present form over many centuries and they offer food for a whole lifetime of human experience and development, not just for the first few years of childhood and adolescence. If some things have therefore been omitted and others given greater emphasis in these readings, this has not been done to falsify the Word of God, but only to allow it to be heard more clearly.

These readings were prepared for children of about ten years and under.[2] Their language was therefore simplified with this age group in mind. The selection of themes was similarly controlled by the demands of modern syllabuses of religious education and by the requirements of the liturgical year as celebrated in a church school. The use of themes, especially of 'secular themes', is a common practice in religious education today. If a child can be led to an appreciation of the things he can see, then there is hope that he can be led on from there to a deeper appreciation of the things of God. This approach can also be a great help in developing the prayer-life of a child within school assemblies, or even within more formal eucharistic liturgies. Indeed the 'secular

[1] Distributed through the Religious Education Centre of the Diocese of Middlesbrough in 1972. I must thank Bishop McClean of Middlesbrough and Father Kilbane of the Centre for the support they gave to this publication.
[2] They have also been found effective in liturgies for mentally handicapped children, and even with the deaf.

168

studies' of a child can become the basis for a more vivid celebration of the whole saving work of Christ.

Clearly these readings allow for a considerable amount of re-working, especially through the use of drama and mime. But even when it is impracticable to 'dramatise' them fully, it is not difficult to divide many of them into playlets with parts for one or two narrators and several characters. The longer readings positively demand some kind of division into several sections, each read by a different child. I think there is also a place for the teacher or leader to draw out the meaning of a particular reading with the help of a short comment after it has been 'performed'. In fact, within a more formal liturgy these readings provide more than enough material for a short homily.

The Catholic *Directory for Masses with Children* makes it clear how important it is for children to learn to read the scriptures for themselves. It therefore specifically recommends the idea of dividing scriptural readings into different parts, in the style of the Readings from the Passion, given during Holy Week in Catholic churches. It encourages the use of introductions before the readings and stresses the value of a homily given afterwards by one of the teachers or by the priestly celebrant himself. Though concerned that the Word of God should not be *obscured* by paraphrases, it nevertheless commends their use so long as there are adequate safeguards against this.[3]

I hope this volume will go some way towards helping children to 'read the Bible for themselves and to understand it and to appreciate more and more the dignity of the Word of God'.

۞

I have used sense lines in these readings to help children read them out loud. Young children often find it very hard to read a continuous slab of prose with understanding or expression. This division of each reading into precise lines has been found to help them locate the natural breaks in the text and to make better sense of it.

Although these texts are not intended to be strictly literal translations, I have given a detailed index of the places where each reading may be located in a full edition of the Bible. I draw attention to the fact that in several readings verses have been re-ordered, and in some cases only part of a verse referred to has been used in the text. References have generally been given according to the Jerusalem Bible, except for the psalms, in which I have followed the Grail Version.

---

[3] See *Directory for Masses with Children*, especially sections 41–8.

NOTES ON THE READINGS

The notes which follow cover a variety of purposes. Some explain the way in which a text has been edited and the reason for this, others comment on the way the readings may be presented, especially within a children's liturgy.

Three general comments apply fairly widely throughout.

(1) I have found the use of music and especially of singing very successful with these readings. Background music can set the mood before the text is read out loud and can even be used to accompany the actual reading itself. A song or psalm, or at least a spoken refrain between the two readings, is much to be encouraged. Several psalms are already provided at various points in the book, some of them with refrains already included, and these could be used with other readings as desired.

(2) In many of the parables Jesus looks forward to the 'End of Time' when the world will be 'harvested' and all things are made new. This eschatological dimension of the New Testament is probably wrongly overlooked by many adults, but is likely to be simply a puzzle to children. In these cases and in others I have often given the moral of the tale as 'God works like that!' and have left it to the teacher or leader to decide for themselves how to apply the story. This is not as strange as it sounds, for there are several levels of appreciation of even the most simple of the stories of Jesus and he was clearly aware of this himself when he used them.

(3) I have not supplied a formal ending to any of these readings largely because there are so many varieties of this from 'Here endeth the Lesson' to 'This is the Gospel of the Lord'. In any case, I do not think they are necessary in children's liturgies, but they can always be introduced into the text if required.

In these notes and in the other lists which follow them, reference numbers refer to theme numbers and the letters refer to the readings in the order which they appear within each theme: e.g. 9(b) refers to the second reading in theme 9.

⌘ *God our Father gives us a wonderful world*

Theme 1 (b) One child can read the verses of the psalm, while everyone else joins in the refrain, 'Thank you, Father . . .'

Theme 2 (a) A different child could read each verse of this, but everyone could join together to say 'and God said it was good' at the end of each section, and the same with 'then God looked . . .' at the very end of the reading.

(b) An example of a reading concerned with the end of time but which also genuinely expresses Christ's own awareness of the beauty of creation.

Theme 3 (a) This introduces the idea of 'death and resurrection within the whole of creation' as a preparation for understanding the death and resurrection of Christ. This makes it a good lenten/springtime reading.

(b) An example of a parable that needs to be 'applied' by the teacher according to the level of development of the children for whom it is intended.

Theme 4 (b) The theme is 'God cares for us all'.

Some people consider the mention of the burning of the flowers goes against the idea of caring and have suggested that the line 'even though they . . .' should be omitted.

Theme 5 (b) This expresses the idea that God is always at work even though we cannot see him.

Theme 6 (a) Here use could be made of recorded music to describe the storm and the floodwaters and then to describe the calm which followed.

Theme 7 (a) Ezekiel was concerned to attack the bad rulers (shepherds) of his own people in this passage, but this does not detract from its use to emphasise the need for children to take good care of their pets since the details given obviously reflect a practical concern with real sheep and not just with the metaphor.

(b) Similarly Jesus himself must have liked the way shepherds 'understood' their animals or he would hardly have used this idea about himself and his human followers.

Theme 8 (b) Jesus clearly loved the birds but not in a sentimental manner. In teaching the moral of this reading it is worth taking care to avoid the image of a soft Jesus surrounded by his pretty little feathered friends!

Theme 9 (b) A reading for winter time when the darkening afternoon hours allow the effective use of candles in a school 'candle ceremony' to demonstrate the idea of Christ the light and to show how he 'shares' his light with all his followers.

Theme 11 (b) Another example of a reading that needs to be 'applied' in a way suitable to the children who are taking part. It may be possible at least to draw attention to the way God allows both good

171

and bad people to live side by side in this world even if we prefer not to consider the 'rewards' they will each receive.

Theme 12 (a) I would not wish to over-emphasise the idea of the burning anger of God so common in the Old Testament. But on the other hand it is worthwhile counter-balancing the idea of God the Father as a sentimental old grand-dad by a reminder of his vigour and strength.

The image of God as a fire or as 'flames' is a good introduction to the notion of God as spirit. The very strength of the 'invisible' flames reminds children of the power of things unseen.

Theme 13 (b) The moral of this story is that Jesus will listen to us when we are in trouble. But it is also desirable to emphasise that we should pray to God in good times as well as in bad.

Also – the followers of Jesus did not speak to him in hushed voices, they talked to him as one person to another (and the Old Testament Psalm treats God the Father in the same way).

Theme 14 (b) By the omission of the whole discussion between Jesus and the Samaritan woman this story has lost its power as one of St John's 'Signs'. But if the story is made familiar to children while they are young, its spiritual content can be filled in later on. In the meantime this reading gives an impression of Jesus 'on the march' and of his friendliness even to strangers.

Theme 15 (a) The second half of this reading can be omitted. The story of Sarah's baby, however, provides a good advent reading with 20c under the title of 'Waiting for a baby'.

The whole of the reading also emphasises the ideas of food as something to be shared with others, food as enjoyable, getting a meal ready, etc.

(b) This introduces the idea of 'making food', i.e. changing the God-given wheat into something different. This can be used to underline the wonderfulness of human co-operation with God the Creator, or it can be employed as an aid in explaining to children how God can change ordinary bread yet again and make it into the eucharist – the bread of life.

Theme 16 God gives us our human life, you could almost say 'God is life' just as we say 'God is love'. In this sense whenever we receive new life from the food we eat, we are receiving God's life yet again. This fact was emphasised at the time of Jesus because ordinary food and drink, like bread and wine, were always 'blessed' before they were eaten. In Jewish eyes even these ordinary things were sacred. All this goes a long way towards explaining to children why Jesus should have chosen bread and wine for the eucharist at the Last Supper.

(b) See theme 36b for a full account of the Last Supper.

Here the words 'This is me' have been used to emphasise more clearly that Jesus means that the eucharistic bread is himself – that he is present in the eucharist. These words merely attempt to isolate this basic meaning of the eucharistic words for teaching purposes.

Theme 17 (a) This reading can remind children that severe deafness affects people's speech and not just their hearing.

Theme 18 These readings can be linked together quite effectively by playing a quiet and gentle piece of music from the point in the first reading where everything becomes still right through to the end of the second reading.

Theme 19 (b) One child can read the verses of the psalm and everyone else can join in the refrain, 'Let's praise him.'

✠ *God our Father gives us his Son, Jesus*

Theme 20 (b) 'We thank you God . . .' can be used as a refrain.

Theme 22 Sub-theme: Jesus comes to give us the chance to become God's children and part of God's family.

Theme 23 Sub-theme: Jesus is the Light of the world.

Theme 24 Sub-theme: People come to see Jesus from the ends of the earth. The reading from Micah could be given to several children to read as if they were a chorus.

Theme 25 (a) 'Sin' is 'going away from God our Father' rather than just breaking a rule.

Theme 26 (b) Jesus had to learn things like other children and no doubt he had to work hard like everyone else.

Theme 27 The baptism of Jesus was unlike the baptism of anyone else. Jesus did not have to be baptised to be 'cleansed from sin' like other people. The baptism of Jesus was the occasion when Jesus began his ministry as the well-loved Son of God the Father and as one who was anointed with the Holy Spirit and with power.

(b) This accordingly emphasises the closeness of the Father and the Son.

Theme 28 Jesus does more than *teach* people about his Father, he effectively *leads* them back to God. And from the very beginning of his ministry he gathers together a group of people who will share this ministry and who will be the basis of the New People of God after his resurrection.

(a) 'to fish for men' – an odd expression that may need explaining to children. It would be a pity to suggest that the followers of Jesus were expected to 'catch' people for Christ – against their will. This expression merely states that the world is full of people waiting for Christ – just like the sea is full of fish. The followers of Jesus can help to bring these people to Christ just as the fishermen help to bring in the fish.

Theme 29 Many Christians have believed throughout the ages that Mary did not give birth to any other children apart from Jesus. It

173

has therefore been suggested that the 'family of Jesus and Mary' was made up of cousins of Jesus or even his half-brothers, adopted by Joseph according to Jewish custom when their own parents had died.

Theme 30 (a) Some writers consider this reading was presented by the early Church as a defence of infant baptism – hence the emphasis given in the second reading.

It may be necessary to explain what it means to 'give someone a blessing'.

(b) This is of course an Old Testament passage dating from a time long before Christian baptism took place. But it gives a remarkable pre-echo of the Christian understanding of baptism by drawing together the following ideas: that God becomes our Father, that he comes to us as an indwelling spirit, that he 'washes' us from our sins, and that we become part of the family of God.

Theme 31 (a) Jesus helps people in all sorts of ways but especially by making them healthy and well.

(b) The Church follows in the footsteps of Jesus.

Theme 32 (a) It does no harm for children to be faced quite early on in life with the realities of sickness and physical/mental handicaps. They need to learn to accept handicapped people into their own society (and indeed they can be more compassionate and understanding than adults).

Theme 33 There are many stories in the Bible about God's holy gift of food but these two linked stories are about the most famous. Jesus was deliberately acting like Moses before him, and St Luke wanted his readers to see that Jesus was also like his Father in heaven for he takes care of the People of God in the same way as his Father.

(b) We also come to Jesus in the eucharist because we are hungry and need to be fed by him. See the Gospel of John (6:9) for details of the boy with the loaves and fish.

Theme 35 A small chorus of children can say (or sing) the Hosanna section, and another (solo) child can read the final sections from Zachariah.

Theme 36 If these readings are too long taken together then the first reading can be omitted or the middle portion of the second reading can be left out (paragraphs 5 and 6) or both.

(b) 'This is my life-blood' – this 'translation' attempts to emphasise the meaning of 'blood' as understood by people long ago. 'Blood' was more than the chemical solution we think of today, it was an expression of the very 'life' of a man which throbbed through his veins. Once again, therefore, Jesus is saying, 'This is me.'

Theme 38 If this shortened version of the passion story is still too long, the last eight lines can be omitted so that the passage ends with the Centurion's words. This is more desirable than to omit the second reading and cut out the reference to the resurrection.

174

Theme 40   Christians also meet Jesus in the breaking of bread in the eucharist, even though other people are unable to recognise him and do not know he is present.

Theme 41   The connection between the Holy Spirit and human breath needs to be explained. Spirit is the word for a blowing wind in Hebrew, Greek and Latin, and God's breath (or spirit) is said to be blowing over the world from the very beginning of time. See the Gospel of Luke (24:36ff.) for details of Jesus eating fish after the resurrection.

Theme 42   Sub-theme: praying is something you can enjoy.

Theme 43   It may be necessary to explain what it means to be 'filled with the Holy Spirit' – perhaps by reminding children that they can be 'full of life' when they are happy, and 'full of the life and breath of God' when they are happy *and* follow Jesus.

Theme 44   Time is not a concept that is grasped accurately by young children, therefore the 'End of Time' suggests a distant and irrelevant thing. More realistic is the idea of 'preparing for the second coming.' These readings also emphasise the universality of Christ's love. 'God is King . . .' can be used as a refrain.

⊞ *We will follow Jesus*

Theme 45   Theme: Jesus is our teacher.
'We will follow God' can be used as a refrain.

Theme 47   (a) The effects of baptism.

Theme 48   (a) Sin=going away from God the Father, thinking only about oneself, being 'stupid', 'walking straight into trouble blindly'. Repentance=waking up to the fact that one is 'in trouble', realising that this is 'stupid', understanding this is one's own fault, making an effort to go back 'home to God', even though ashamed of oneself.
Forgiveness=the Father's welcome to the sinful child, the Father's willingness to go out and meet his son, the Father's happiness and readiness to make his son feel at home again, the celebration of the rest of the family at the son's return.
Sin=death.   Repentance and forgiveness=resurrection.
   (b) 'Lord I am sorry' can be used as a refrain.

Theme 49   (a) The 'test' in the last line is the 'trial of the End of Time' before the second coming. This may not be very realistic to the children, who may even think that God must be rather cruel to 'test' anyone. It is necessary therefore to show how it is necessary to test a plank to see if it will take a heavy weight, to take an exam to see if someone is safe enough to drive a car, etc. God obviously wants to see if people are good enough because they are more important than a plank of wood or a piece of driving. But we still pray that God will not make our test too hard because sometimes we feel very weak.

Theme 51 (a) Even Jesus cannot do just as he likes.

Theme 61 The cruel destructiveness of human death can be felt very strongly even by a young child. It is therefore good to present the Christian understanding of death from the very start.

⊠ *We are the family of God*

Theme 62 Sub-theme: Trust of God.
'Blessed be God' can be used as a response.

Theme 63 Sub-theme: God cares for us.

Theme 64 Sub-theme: Prayer.
Prayer means many different things, being quiet with God as with our parents at night, 'talking to God' and knowing he always listens, remembering all the good things God our Father has done for us and saying 'thank you', saying 'sorry' when we have done wrong, etc.

Theme 65 Sub-theme: Closeness to God.

Theme 66 Sub-theme: Courage.

Theme 67 Sub-theme: Friendship.
(a) See 1 Samuel 19:8ff. for another version of this story, giving more details of Saul's attempt to kill David, of David's escape and of Jonathan's 'arrow signals'.

Theme 68 Sub-theme: Helping people to come to God.

Theme 69 Sub-theme: Doing what God wants.

Theme 70 Sub-theme: Staying close to Jesus.
(a) Mary, the Mother of Jesus, was a real mother and she did not like to see her son hurt, but she tried to help him as much as she could by staying close to him when he was dying.
(b) Mary obviously stayed very close to God by praying.

Theme 71 Sub-theme: Staying close to Jesus.

Theme 72 Sub-theme: Betraying Jesus.

Theme 73 Sub-theme: Forgiveness.
(b) Explain the Jewish hatred of the Jewish tax man who worked for the Romans.

Theme 74 Sub-theme: Jesus welcomes the sinner.

Theme 75 Sub-theme: Obedience.

Theme 76 Sub-theme: Faith.

Theme 77 Sub-theme: Forgiveness.

Theme 78 Sub-theme: Baptism.

Theme 79 Sub-theme: The way of the cross.
(a) See Acts 27 for the story of the shipwreck.
Acts 16:19 for the story of Paul arrested and beaten.
Acts 9:20 for the story of Paul's escape.

Theme 80 Sub-theme: We must forgive others.

Theme 81 Sub-theme: Baptism.

Theme 82 Sub-theme: Christians are like Christ.

LIST OF PEOPLE AND PLACES[1]

Abraham 12a, 15a, 62ac
Ananias 78a
Andrew, one of the twelve 28a, 28
Anna 25b
Antioch 82b
Bethlehem 22, 23b, 24, 63b, 65a, 66a
Calvary, *see* Hill of the Skull
Capernaum 76b
Children of God 1c, 8a, 22a, 47a, 62a
Damascus 78a
David, King 65a, 66a, 67a
Egypt 12a, 14a, 36a, 63ab
Eli, the teacher of Samuel 64a
Elijah 18a
Elizabeth 69a
Emmaus 40a
Ethiopia 81b
followers of Jesus (including friends of Jesus) 13b, 14b, 19c, 30a, 34b, 40a, 42a, 43b, 44c, 45c, 47b, 49a, 50b, 60b, 61b, 65b, 70b, 78a, 80b, 81a, 82b
Galilee 14b, 39b, 72b, 81a
God the Father, see especially 1bc, 2a, 8a, 16b, 19a, 22a, 26ab, 27ab, 29b, 30b, 34a, 38b, 39a, 40b, 42a, 43a, 44a, 45a, 46a, 49a, 51a, 55b, 61a, 62c, 64b, 65b, 71b, 78b, 83
Goliath 66a
Herod, King 24, 63b
Hill of the Skull (Calvary) 38a, 77b
Holy Spirit 25b, 27a, 30b, 41a, 43ab, 47a, 49b, 77a, 78a, 80b, 82b
Isaac 12a, 15a
Jacob 12a
Jacob's well 14b
Jairus 31a
James, one of the twelve 28a, 31a, 37a, 52b
Jericho 10a, 56b, 74b
Jerusalem 19c, 24, 25b, 26b, 32b, 35, 36b, 42a, 43b, 50b, 56b, 66b, 70b, 81b
Jesus, the life story, see 20–44;
escape into Egypt 63b; calls Matthew 73b; preaches at home 69b; sends out the twelve 67b; baptises 81a; calls Zachaeus 74b; the twelve stay with Jesus 71a; enters Jerusalem 19c; in Jerusalem before his death 66b; is arrested 72b; on the cross 70a; dies 77b; after the ascension 70b

[1] Thanks are due to Sister Mary Therese Martin and Sister Mary Margaret Henson for their work on these word lists.

177

LIST OF TOPICS AND WORDS

afternoon 15a

anger 18a, 30a, 48c, 51a, 54b, 62c, 63b, 73a, 77a

animals (*including* sheep, wild animals, crawling things) 2a, 6a, 7ab, 12a, 23b, 24a, 36a, 66a, 74a, 79a

arguments 18a, 48c, 58a, 60b

arms 25b, 30a, 31ab

arrest 37a, 72b, 80b

ashamed 72b

ask (prayer) 10a, 13abc, 14a, 17, 31ab, 32ab, 49a, 50b, 58bc, 60a, 64b, 65b, 66b, 75b, 77b

astonish 31a, 76b

baby 15a, 20c, 21a, 22b, 24a, 63a, 69a

bake 11a, 15ab

bandit 56b, 77b, 79b

baptism 27a, 47a, 78ab, 81ab, 82a

barn 2b, 11b

beach 1a, 3c

beauty 2b, 4b, 12a, 63a

bed 64a, 79b

beggar 10a, 32b, 83

believe 29a, 31a, 41b, 62ac, 71a, 76b, 82a

betray (let down) 13b, 14a, 24, 36b, 38a, 66b, 69a, 72b

bible 25b, 40a, 56a, 81b

birds 2a, 3ac, 6ab, 8b, 27a, 72b, 79a

birth 15a, 22, 23, 24, 57a, 63a

bless 16b, 17a, 25b, 30a, 33b, 36b, 40a, 41b, 42a, 65a, 78a, 80b

blindness 10a, 64a, 78a

boat (*and* ship) 3c, 6a, 13b, 28a, 52b, 79b

body 36b, 38a, 40a, 59b

bread 11a, 15ab, 16ab, 33b, 36ab, 52b, 66a

breath 20b, 41a

brothers 28a, 51b, 53b, 69b

burn 4ab, 11ab, 36a

buy 8b, 14b, 33b, 48a

candle 9b

care for 1c, 4b, 7a, 8ab, 46b, 53ab, 58b, 60b, 62b, 70a, 80b

carefulness 4b, 59b

cave 18a, 38a, 39b

chariot 81b

cheat 74b

cheerfulness 59b

children 26b, 30a, 31ab, 32a, 47a, 63b, 64a, 65a

choose 20a, 47b, 71b

Christians 82b

church (building), *see* Temple, *in* List of People and Places

church (people), *see* children of God, followers of Jesus, *in* List of People and Places

clap 44b

clean 14a, 30b

closeness to God 25ab, 27b, 42b, 54a, 60a, 61b, 65a, 78b

clothes 4b, 18a, 22b, 23b, 35a, 39b, 48a, 56b, 57a, 58ac, 59a, 67a, 68b

colour 2b, 3b, 23a, 65a

complain 33a, 46b, 71a, 73b, 74b

cook 15a, 33a, 36a, 52b

cost 8b, 56b

count 1a, 62a

courage 66ab

creation 1ab, 2a

cripple 32b, 76b

crops (*including* corn, wheat) 2ab, 5b, 11b

cross (*including* sign of the cross) 38a, 77b, 78b

crowds 13b, 17a, 33b, 35a, 37b, 38a, 69b

crying 31a, 72b

cup 16b, 36b

dance 19b

darkness (*see also* night time) 9a, 10b, 21a, 23a, 25a, 31b, 40a, 54a, 62a

dawn 23a, 39b, 52b

day 1b, 2a, 4a, 42b

deafness 17a

death 13a, 25b, 31ab, 32a, 38ab, 39a, 57a, 61ab, 66a, 77b

denial 72b

depth 1a, 13a, 54a

desert 12a, 18a, 33a, 62a

difficulties 11b, 13abc, 34b, 49b, 71a

distance 1a, 54a

door 41a, 76b

doubt 15a, 41a

drink 14ab, 18a, 58c

drown 6a, 13ab

dryness 3c, 4a

dumbness 17a

ear 17a, 80b

earth 1b, 2a, 19c, 23b, 44bc

eat 5a, 12a, 18a, 31a, 33ab, 36ab

emptiness 9a

enemy 11b, 66a, 82b

escape 12a, 18a, 36a, 63b, 79b

boy who has fits 32a; calming of the storm 13b; catch of fish 52b; centurion's servant 75b; deaf man who could not speak 17a; feeding of the crowds 33b; Jairus' daughter 31a; man who came in through the roof 76b; man who could not walk (Peter) 32b; ten lepers 50b

money 32b, 48a, 54b, 55b, 56b, 57ab, 58c, 59b, 73b, 74b, 82b

moon 1b, 2a

morning 14b, 23a, 39b, 40a, 52b, 72b

mother 20c, 22ab, 24, 31a, 63ab, 69b, 70a

mountain 7a, 18a. *See also* Sinai *in* List of People and Places

music (*including* musical instruments) 19b, 44b, 67a. *See also* sing

name 2a, 7b, 19c, 28b, 32b, 64a, 77a

neighbour 45b, 56a

nest 6b, 79a

nets 28a, 52b

night 1b, 4a, 5b, 11b, 13b, 18a, 23a, 26b, 37b, 41a, 42b, 52b, 56b, 66b, 79b. *See also* darkness

noise 13b. *See also* sound

nuisance 31a, 75b

numbers 14a, 50b, 54b, 74ab, 80a, 82b

obey 5a, 6a, 20c, 22a, 25b, 27b, 30b, 37ab, 44a, 46a, 47b, 64b, 69b, 75ab, 78a

oil 65a

old people 15a, 25b, 64a

parables: banquet 83; bread making 15b; builders 46a; Dives and Lazarus 58a; flowers 4b; Good Samaritan 56b; light 9b; lost sheep 74a; mustard seed 6b; Prodigal Son 48a; rich man and poor man 58c; seed 5b; sower 3c; sparrows 8b; talents 54b; two sons 75a; unforgiving servant 55b; weeds 11b

parents 25b, 31b

passover meal 36ab

patience 48c, 50a

pay back 55b

perfume 3a

pity 48a, 55b, 56b, 63a

politeness 72a

poor people 57b, 58ac, 69a, 74b, 83

praise 19bc, 20b, 26a, 32b, 42b, 44b, 49a, 50b, 69a

prayer 10b, 17a, 32a, 37a, 38a, 49ab, 50a, 53b, 58a, 60a, 62b, 64b, 66b, 70b, 78a, 80b. *See also* ask

preaching 28b, 29a, 31b, 43b, 66b, 79b, 82a

pretend 53b, 82b

priest 24a, 34a, 37b, 50b, 56b, 64a

prison 37b, 55b, 78a, 79b, 80b

promise 21b, 24, 56b, 62a, 77b

183

winter 3a
wisdom 1ab, 26b, 29a, 67a, 80b
words 49b
work 20a, 47b, 48a, 51b, 53b, 59b, 73b, 79ab
worry 4b, 8b, 18b, 20a, 26b, 31a, 57a, 64b, 74a
wound 41ab, 56b
wrong-doing 25a, 29b, 45ab, 46b, 48b, 49a, 68b, 72a, 77b, 80ab
yeast 15b

OTHER THEMES

Many of the entries in the List of People and Places, and the List of Topics and Words suggest other themes. Here we give a few examples of new themes.

Some of them use existing groupings of readings, and merely involve renaming the group, and perhaps rewriting its introduction. Other themes may be created by regrouping the passages completely.

Advent: the Annunciation 20; waiting for a baby 15a(ii) and 20c; John the Baptist 21 and 68; the birth of Jesus 22 and 23;
Lent: Ash Wednesday 59b (working for Jesus) and 78b (the sign of the cross); Jesus is going to die 34; prayer 49; forgiveness 48; doing our best 54; Palm Sunday 35; Jesus is arrested 37
Special times
    beginning of the year 53
    end of the year 45
    Mother's Day 22a or 63a and 26b (Mothers have a lot of worries)
    Father's Day 8a and 27b
    birthdays 17b and 19b and 23b (up to end paragraph 3)
    first Holy Communion 16
    holidays 52 or 47
Other themes
    God loves everyone all over the world 43b and 44c
    Jesus is the greatest, Jesus is the Son of God 39a and 29b and 19c
    Jesus loves us with all his heart 30b and 27b
    the People of God should love each other (Christian Unity) 47b and 45c
    we must all live in peace 50a and 18b
    it's wonderful to be able to learn 1a and 26b
    we must keep God's rules 53a and 56a
    rich people should help poorer people 58

186

WHERE TO FIND THE THEMES IN YOUR BIBLE

⊕ *God our Father gives us a wonderful world*

1 God is wise, God is kind
 Ecclesiasticus 1:1.2.3.10
 Psalm 135:1.5.6.8.9
 Matthew 5:45
2 The world is good
 Genesis 1:9.10.6.14.16.11.
 20.24.26.31
 John 4:35.36
3 Flowers are beautiful
 Song of Songs 2:11.12.13.12
 Psalm 1:3
 Mark 4:1.3–8
4 Flowers don't worry about anything!
 Isaiah 27:3.4.6
 Luke 12:27.28
5 God makes everything grow
 Leviticus 26:3–5
 Mark 4:26–28
6 God takes care of the animals
 Genesis 6:19–21. link 8:6–
 12.16.17.20
 Mark 4:30–33
7 The shepherd and his sheep
 Ezekiel 34:3–6
 John 10:3–5.14
8 Sparrows don't cost much!
 1 John 3:1.4.7.8
 Luke 12:6.7
9 Let there be light!
 Genesis 1:1–3
 Matthew 5:14–15
10 Blind men can't see!
 Luke 18:35–43
 Psalm 17:2.4.29

11 Don't touch the fire, or you'll
 get burnt!
 Isaiah 48:14
 Matthew 13:24–30
12 The Fire of God
 Exodus 3:1–8
 Luke 12:49
13 Help, Lord, we're drowning!
 Psalm 68:2.3.15.16
 Mark 4:35–41
 Psalm 43:24.25.27
14 Water, water everywhere and
 not a drop to drink!
 Exodus 15:22–25.27
 John 4:3.6–8. link 27.28
15 Food, glorious food!
 Genesis 18:1–2.4–8.10.12.
 14. 21:2–3
 Matthew 13:33
16 Bread from heaven
 John 6:32.33.35.55.56
 1 Corinthians 11:24–27
17 It's good to hear and good to
 speak
 Mark 7:32–36
 Isaiah 12:4–6
18 The Sound of God
 1 Kings 18:46. 19:3–5.8.9.
 11–13
 John 14:27
19 Make music and praise God
 Colossians 3:12.16.17
 Psalm 150:2–6
 Luke 19:37–38

⊕ *God our Father gives us his Son, Jesus*

20 A message from God
 Isaiah 41:9.10
 Psalm 99:1–5
 Luke 1:26–31.38

21 Waiting for Jesus
 Isaiah 9:1.2.6.7
 Luke 3:10.11.14–16

22 Jesus is born in Bethlehem
   Galatians 4:4–6
   Luke 2:4–7
23 The shepherds come to Jesus
   Isaiah 60:2a.1.2b
   Luke 2:7–20
24 The wise men come to Jesus
   Matthew 2:1–5
   Micah 5:1–4
   Matthew 2:8–12
25 Simeon and Anna
   1 John 1:5–7
   Luke 2:23.22.25.28–30.32–
   34.37–39
26 Jesus goes to the Temple School
   Psalm 145:4–6.8
   Luke 2:41–51.40
27 Jesus is baptised
   Mark 1:9–11
   John 15:10b.9.10a.14:21–23
28 Jesus and 'The Twelve'
   Mark 1:16–20. 3:13–19
29 Jesus goes back to Nazareth
   Mark 6:1–4
   Ephesians 1:3.6.5.4
30 Jesus makes the children wel-
   come
   Mark 10:13.14.16
   Ezekiel 36:24–28
31 Jesus looks after a little girl
   Mark 5:22–24.35–43
   Acts 20:7–12
32 Jesus looks after a little boy
   Mark 9:17–27
   Acts 3:1–9
33 Jesus looks after the people who
   follow him
   Exodus 16:3.4.14.17

Leviticus 11:8
   Luke 9:11–17
34 Jesus says he is going to die
   Mark 8:27–33
   Philippians 3:8.10
35 Palm Sunday
   Matthew 21:1–3.6–9
   Zechariah 9:9
36 The Last Supper
   Exodus 12:3.4.8–11
   Mark 14:12–20.22–26
37 Jesus is arrested!
   Mark 14:32–37.39–46
   Acts 4:1.3.5.7.10
38 Good Friday
   Mark 15:12–21.24.29.34
   Psalm 22:1.20.23.25
   Mark 15:37.39.43.46
   Acts 2:22.23.32
39 Easter Sunday
   Ephesians 1:20.22.21
   Mark 16:2–8
40 Jesus is alive!
   Luke 24:13–33
   1 Corinthians 15:3–8
41 Doubting Thomas
   John 20:19–23.24–29
42 Jesus goes back to his Father
   Luke 24:50–53
   Psalm 15:7–9
43 Jesus sends the Holy Spirit
   John 16:5.7.13
   Acts 2:2–4
44 We will see Jesus again
   Philippians 3:20.21. 4:1
   Psalm 46:2.3.6.8
   Mark 13:9.26.27

✂ *We will follow Jesus*

45 Jesus tells us what to do
   1 John 4:9.10
   Psalm 14:2.3
   John 15:11.12.15
46 We will listen to Jesus
   Matthew 7:21.24–27
   Leviticus 19:16–18

47 'You are my friends'
   Titus 3:4–7
   John 15:15–17
48 'I have forgiven you!'
   Luke 15:11–32
   Colossians 3:12.13
49 'Teach us to pray!'

188

Luke 11:1–4
Romans 8:26–27
50 'Thank you, God!'
1 Thessalonians 5:12–18
Luke 17:11–19
51 'Working for Jesus'
John 5:17.19.30.36
Romans 8:28.29
52 'Enjoy yourselves!'
Ecclesiastes 11:8–10
John 21:2–6.9.10.12
53 The New Rule
John 13:34.35
Romans 12:8.10.13.11.12
54 'Do your best!
Psalm 138:1–6.8.9.11
Luke 19:12.13.15–22
55 'Forgive your brother!'
Ecclesiasticus 28:3–5
Matthew 18:23–35

56 The kindness of a stranger
Luke 10:26.30–37
57 The poor old woman
1 Timothy 6:6.7.10
Mark 12:41–44
58 A rich man goes to hell
Isaiah 58:3.4.7.8
Psalm 71:12–14
Luke 16:19–26
59 'When were *you* ill, Jesus?'
Matthew 25:34–40
Romans 12:4.5.8
60 'Stop arguing!'
Isaiah 58:9.11.9
Mark 9:33–35
61 'Don't be sad'
1 Thessalonians 4:13.14.17.
15
John 14:1–3

⊞ *We are the family of God*

62 Abraham trusted God
Genesis 12:2.7. link 15:5.6.
12.17.18
Psalm 27:6.7
John 8:39–40
63 Moses was nearly killed!
Exodus 1:8.9.12 2:2–10
Matthew 2:13.16.14
64 Samuel: the boy who listened to God
1 Samuel 3:2–9.19
Matthew 6:31–33
65 David: the boy who looked after the sheep
1 Samuel 16:7.10–13
John 17:11–13
66 David and Goliath
1 Samuel 17:12–14.17.18.
20–24.28.31–35.45.49.52
Luke 21:37.36.38
67 David and Jonathan
1 Samuel 16:17–19.21
18:1.3–5 19:1–4.6.7
Mark 6:6.7.30–32

68 John the Baptist
Isaiah 40:3–5
Matthew 3:5.4.2.6
69 Mary and Elizabeth
Luke 1:36.39–43.46–55.
Mark 3:20.21.31–35
70 Mary knows how to pray
John 19:25–27
Acts 1:13.14
71 The friends of Jesus stay with him
John 6:60.61.66–68
1 Thessalonians 1:4–6
72 Saint Peter tells a lie
Titus 3:3.4.2
Matthew 26:57.58.69–75
73 Saint Matthew, the tax-man
Joel 2:12.13
Matthew 9:9–11.13
74 A rich man called Zachaeus
Luke 15:4–7.19:1–8
75 The soldier who did as he was told
Matthew 21:28–31
Luke 7:2–10

76 The man who came in through the roof
Jeremiah 30:10.12.13.17
Mark 2:1–6.11.12
77 The good thief
Ephesians 4:25.26.31.32
Luke 23:33.35.34.38–43.46
78 The baptism of Saint Paul
Matthew 28:19–20
Acts 9:1–5.8.11.12.17
79 'The hard life!'
Luke 9:57.58
2 Corinthians 11:23.25–27. 32.33. 12:10

80 Saint Stephen forgave the people who killed him
Luke 17:3.4
Acts 6:2–6.8.10–12. 7:57. 59.60
81 Saint Philip and the man in a chariot
Acts 8:26–30.34–38
82 'A priest called Joseph Barnabas'
Mark 16:15.16.20
Acts 4:36–37. 9:26–27. 11:23.24.26
83 Everyone is welcome in the People of God!
Luke 14:16–21. 24.22–23

WHERE TO FIND PASSAGES FROM THE BIBLE IN THIS BOOK

ABOUT THE AUTHOR

Sanjay Deshpande

The author, an archaeologist and heritage consultant, was born in 1965 in Nagpur, India. He grew up in Mumbai (formerly known as Bombay), but spent his formative years in the Philippines and then USA. He later went to the Universities of Toronto and Texas where he specialised in the search for oil and gas.

In 1992, he was offered the opportunity to excavate as part of the Archaeological Survey of India's excavation at the 5000-year-old Harappan Civilisation city of Dholavira on the island of Khadir in the Great Rann of Kutch. He excavated at Dholavira till 1998 and dug out parts of the city, the citadel, and the cemetery complex, as well as parts of the reservoir system, including a water storage tank and a dam.

After getting married in 1999 to a fellow archaeologist, Deshpande and his wife joined the joint Deccan College and University of Pennsylvania team excavating at the Ahar Culture site of Gilund (2500–1700 BC), where they found many new facets of that culture. The most important of these include the presence of a written script, the oldest *tandoor* (clay oven), the oldest 'Nandi' bull figurine, and a beautifully maintained road with wheel tracks and repaired potholes.

Since 1999, he has also been actively working to promote, preserve, and protect the vast cultural and natural heritage in and around the city of Pune where he lives. He is also an active photographer and trekker who enjoys exploring new places.

INDUS VALLEY

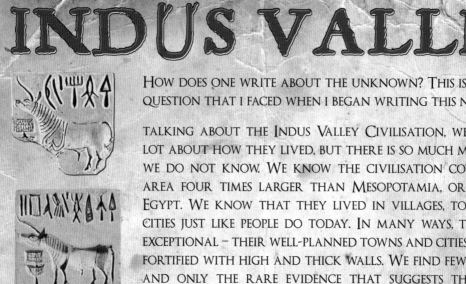

How does one write about the unknown? This is the very question that I faced when I began writing this novel.

Talking about the Indus Valley Civilisation, we know a lot about how they lived, but there is so much more that we do not know. We know the civilisation covered an area four times larger than Mesopotamia, or Ancient Egypt. We know that they lived in villages, towns, and cities just like people do today. In many ways, they were exceptional – their well-planned towns and cities were all fortified with high and thick walls. We find few weapons and only the rare evidence that suggests that there may have been warfare. Similarly, there is little evidence of poverty, which surely must have been there. Unlike all their contemporaries, Harappan cities had proper sewage systems – a feature that was to become commonplace elsewhere only 3,500 years after their world collapsed around 2000 BC! We have found evidence that the people were craftsmen, farmers, traders, and animal herders. They built dams, had rain water harvesting systems, and complex domestic and international trade networks that stretched throughout South Asia, the Middle East, and as far as Egypt.

Interestingly, while the entire Harappan world had a uniform system of weights, planned cities and towns, standardised types of pottery, seals, script, and construction bricks, which speak of authority and control, there is practically nothing known about their rulers. While their neighbouring rulers were building pyramids, temples, great monuments, and filling their graves with their land's gold, the Harappan rulers did nothing of the sort. No great monuments, palaces, temples, or graveyards full of gold have been found. It is as if the concept of a ruler and the ruled was completely different there. Unfortunately, their written records, which could have shed some light on this, seem to have been written mostly on perishable materials. And whatever writing has been found is all on personal artefacts and has not been deciphered yet.

CIVILISATION

All this means that with the exception of Sargon, all the characters in the story are fictional. In fact, we do not even know what the Indus Valley people called themselves or their cities. Perhaps the invasion happened – after all Sargon did boast that he had made the boats of Dilmun (Bahrain), Magan (UAE/Oman), and Meluha (Indus Civilisation) dock at the ports of Akkad. But in truth, we do not know. The rest of the material in the novel – the ships, cities, countryside, markets, the religious customs, the stuff of everyday life – is, however, all exactly as archaeologists believe it to have been then.

A few final points: the horse may or may not have been present – the evidence is disputed; the story of the comet derives from the belief among some scientists that around 3100 BC a large meteor or comet slammed into the Indian Ocean and may have marked a period of great tumult and disaster.

AT TORANA'S ASHRAM NEAR VARANASI. 150 BC.

I WONDER WHAT MASTER TORANA IS GOING TO TEACH US TODAY?

I LOVED THE LAST LESSON ABOUT ALEXANDER'S BATTLE WITH RAJA RAI POR. IT MADE ME FEEL SO PROUD.

WHEN I RULE, I WILL BE A GREAT KING JUST LIKE HIM.

WE WILL CONQUER ALL OUR NEIGHBOURS!

TOGETHER WE WILL RULE THE WORLD!

IT SEEMS MY STUDENTS NEED TO BE TAUGHT THAT WAR IS NOT ALWAYS THE ONLY, OR THE BEST, SOLUTION TO CONFLICT.

THEY NEED A LESSON IN WHICH A BATTLE IS WON THROUGH STRATEGY, WITH MINIMAL LOSS OF LIFE. THAT WOULD HELP THEM THINK RATIONALLY BEFORE TAKING ANY DECISION.

PRINCES, TODAY WE ARE GOING TO LEARN A DIFFERENT TACTIC. I AM GOING TO TELL YOU ABOUT A WAR THAT WAS WON BY STRATEGY WITH ONLY A FEW SOLDIERS. A WAR BETWEEN THE HARAPPANS AND THE MIGHTY AKKADIANS. A WAR THAT BEGAN...

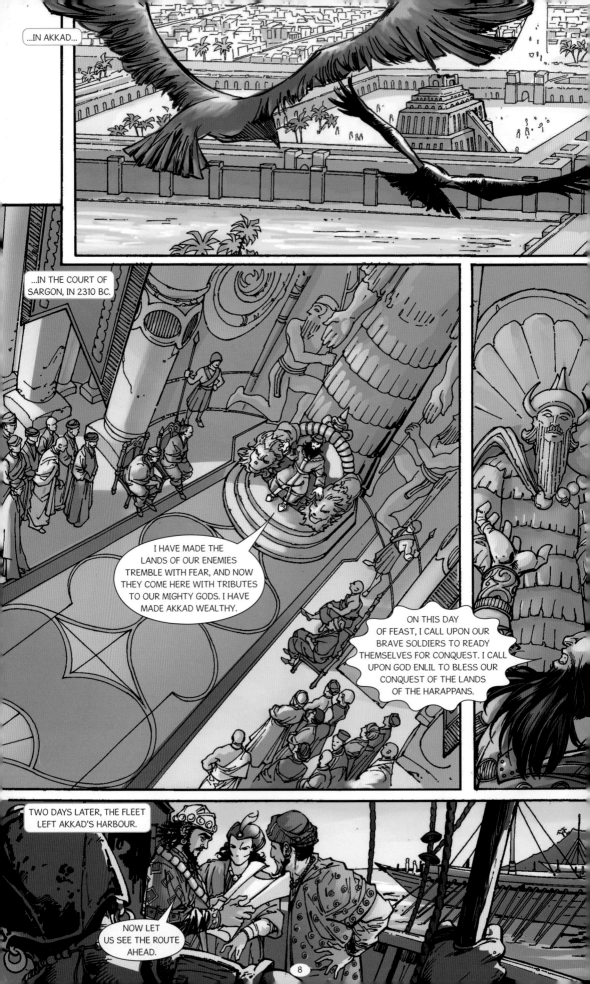

EIGHT HUNDRED YEARS AGO, A GROUP OF REFUGEES LED BY RAJA DHOLA, FLED SIND TO ESCAPE THE FAMINE THAT HAD STRUCK THE LAND BEFORE THE GREAT COMET HIT THE EARTH.

FOR THREE DAYS, THEY WERE LOST. JUST WHEN THEY THOUGHT THAT THEY WOULD NOT SURVIVE ANOTHER NIGHT, THEY SAW A LIGHT – A BEACON IN THE NIGHT.

THEY WERE GUIDED BY THAT LIGHT TO THIS SPOT WHERE THEY SAW A TREE STRUCK BY PASHUPATI'S THUNDERBOLT. AT THE FOOT OF THE TREE, THERE WAS A POOL OF FRESH WATER.

IT WAS THEN THAT RAJA DHOLA, REACHING DOWN FOR A HANDFUL OF WATER, SAW PASHUPATI HIMSELF. HE KNEW INSTANTLY THAT THIS WAS THE PLACE WHERE THEY WERE DESTINED TO LIVE.

WITH THE WATER FROM THIS SACRED POND, MAY PASHUPATI WASH AWAY YOUR SINS, AND GUIDE YOUR FOOTSTEPS FROM THIS DAY ONWARDS.

TIRED, THEY REACHED SARAN LATE IN THE DAY.

YOUR HIGHNESS! A MESSENGER HAS COME LOOKING FOR YOU. HE SAYS HE CARRIES A MESSAGE FROM YOUR FATHER. HE IS WAITING FOR YOU IN THE COMMANDANT'S OFFICE.

YOUR HIGHNESS, THIS IS THE MAN WHO CLAIMS TO HAVE BEEN SENT BY YOUR FATHER. WE HAVE SEARCHED HIM; HE CARRIES NO WEAPONS OR MESSAGE.

SIR, PERMIT ME TO PROVE THAT I AM, INDEED, SENT BY YOUR FATHER. I BEAR HIS INSIGNIA ON MY SHOULDER.

MY FATHER'S INSIGNIA!

QUICK, MESSENGER! TELL ME WHAT MY FATHER WISHES FROM ME!

HE ALSO TELLS YOU THAT THE ARMY OF SARGON IS TOO LARGE FOR THE CITY TO HOLD OUT FOR MORE THAN A MONTH OR TWO. HE FEARS THAT ALL OF KUTCH WILL SOON BE UNDER ATTACK.

HIS HIGHNESS HAS ASKED ME TO TELL YOU THAT THE CITY IS SURROUNDED, AND UNDER NO CONDITIONS SHOULD YOU TRY TO RETURN.

HE WANTS THE TWO OF YOU TO GO NORTH TO MOHENJO-DARO AND ON TO HARAPPA, AND SEND HELP. HE WANTS YOU TO ASK THEM TO FIGHT TOGETHER, UNITED AS ONE PEOPLE AGAINST A COMMON ENEMY.

17

THERE, PRINCE, IS THE WESTERNMOST BRANCH OF THE SINDHU'S DELTA. WE WILL SAIL UP THIS CHANNEL UNTIL WE COME TO THE MAIN RIVER. THEN WE SHALL MOVE TO LAL DARO, THE FORT THAT CONTROLS ACCESS TO SIND.

LET US STOP HERE AND WALK THE REST OF THE WAY.

WHY? DO YOU SUSPECT TROUBLE?

LAL DARO'S IMPORTANCE IS WELL KNOWN. WHO KNOWS WHAT LIES AHEAD? OUR ENEMY IS BOUND TO HAVE PEOPLE WATCHING THIS AREA.

SMOKE! LOTS OF IT! YOUR CAUTION, IT SEEMS, WAS WELL WARRANTED!

BE ON YOUR GUARD. THE LAST TIME I WAS HERE, THE AREA WAS TEEMING WITH FISHERMEN. TODAY THERE IS NOBODY. SOMETHING IS DEFINITELY AMISS.

LAL DARO HAS FALLEN TO SARGON'S FORCES. I FEAR THE GATES OF OUR LAND ARE NOW WIDE OPEN FOR THE ENEMY TO ENTER AT WILL.

THERE, MY PRINCE, LIES THE DRY BED OF THE NARA RIVER. ALL WE HAVE TO DO IS FOLLOW ITS OLD COURSE TO THE HEARTLAND OF SIND AND MOHENJO-DARO.

FINE. WE SHALL START TOMORROW. LET US REST TONIGHT WITH THOSE GOAT HERDERS.

WELCOME TO OUR CAMP. HOW CAN WE HELP YOU?

WE HAVE A LONG JOURNEY AHEAD OF US, AND WISH TO SPEND THE NIGHT HERE. WILL YOU BE ABLE TO ACCOMMODATE US IN YOUR CAMP?

YES, SIR. AND YOU ARE ALSO WELCOME TO SHARE OUR HUMBLE MEAL WITH US.

TELL ME, WHERE ARE YOU FROM AND WHERE ARE YOU GOING?

LORD, WE COME FROM THE MOUNTAINS TO THE FAR WEST, A MONTH'S JOURNEY AWAY. EVERY WINTER, OUR PEOPLE DESCEND AND SCATTER OVER THE PLAINS, LOOKING FOR FOOD FOR OUR HERDS.

LAST YEAR, WE HEARD OF A FAR-OFF LAND WHERE MANY GREAT RIVERS FLOW TO THE EAST ACROSS THE DESERT.

BACK AT OUR CITY, WHICH LIES ON THE OTHER SIDE OF THE RANN OF KUTCH, THOSE LIKE YOU ARE ALL LOCAL PEOPLE. BUT HERE IN THE DESERT?

WE DECIDED TO TRAVEL THERE TO FATTEN OUR GOATS AND OURSELVES. AND HERE WE ARE.

I KNOW THE LAND YOU SPEAK OF – IT IS CALLED MALWA AND LIES A FORTNIGHT AWAY IN THE DIRECTION OF SUNRISE FROM HERE.

BUT WHATEVER YOU DO, DO NOT GO WEST RIGHT NOW AS WAR IS UPON THE LAND.

23

MAY I ASK YOU WHY YOU WERE PATROLLING IN THIS AREA SPECIFICALLY?

I WONDER IF THIS WAS THE REASON WHY I HAVE BEEN FEELING THAT SOMEONE HAS BEEN WATCHING US SINCE YESTERDAY. I HAD BETTER KEEP A SHARPER EYE OUT FROM NOW ON.

MY LORD, WE HAVE BEEN GETTING REPORTS OF STRANGERS ON CAMELS ROAMING THESE RIDGES. WHAT IS WORRYING IS THAT THEY RIDE AWAY WHEN HAILED.

SOLDIER, USE THE SIGNAL FLAG TO GET FAST TRANSPORT FROM THE FORT SO THAT OUR GUESTS CAN BE TAKEN QUICKLY TO MOHENJO-DARO. TELL THEM WE WILL MEET THEM ON THE ROAD BELOW.

SOME TIME LATER.

YOUR TRANSPORT APPROACHES, LORDS.

CHANDRAYAAN, THEY ARE APPROACHING VERY FAST EVEN FOR WELL-BRED BULLOCKS, DON'T YOU THINK SO?

I DO BELIEVE THEY ARE--

HORSES!

PRAISE THE GODS! THEY ARE MAGNIFICENT!

I HAD HEARD RUMOURS THAT RAJA SUSHANA HAD IMPORTED MANY OF THEM FOR HIS ARMY, BUT TO SEE THEM IN FLESH IS AMAZING!

THIS CHARIOT WILL TAKE YOU TO MOHENJO-DARO. YOU SHOULD BE THERE WITHIN A FEW HOURS.

THANK YOU VERY MUCH. I SHALL REMEMBER YOUR HELP AND REWARD YOU WHEN THE TIME COMES.

27

BEFORE PEOPLE SETTLED ON THESE PLAINS, WE USED TO BE HIGHLAND PEOPLE LIKE THOSE HERDERS WE MET A FEW DAYS AGO.

A FEW WISE MEN LEFT THE HILLS WITH THOSE WHO WOULD FOLLOW AND MOVED DOWN TO THESE PLAINS.

THESE MEN ALSO ACTED AS HEALERS AND PRIESTS, AND LATER BECAME KINGS.

OVER TIME, THEY BUILT DAMS, IRRIGATION CHANNELS, AND ROADS. VILLAGES BECAME TOWNS AND THEN CITIES. AND THE LAND PROSPERED.

MOHENJO-DARO, LOCATED IN THE MIDST OF THIS GREAT FLOOD PLAIN, BECAME THE CAPITAL. AND ITS LORD, THROUGH CONQUEST, BECAME AN EMPEROR RULING OUR ENTIRE REALM.

CHANDRAYAAN, PLEASE TELL ME ABOUT THESE GREAT KINGS WHOM YOU PRAISE SO HIGHLY. I WOULD LIKE TO LEARN FROM THEM.

MY LORDS...

...WE HAVE REACHED!

YOUR HIGHNESS, THE TROUBLES BEGAN LESS THAN A WEEK AGO WHEN, ONE MORNING, WE WOKE UP TO FIND THE SEA COVERED WITH AKKADIAN SHIPS. FORTUNATELY, CHANDRAYAAN AND I WERE OUT OF THE CITY HUNTING.

WE TRIED TO RETURN, BUT THE CITY WAS ALREADY UNDER SIEGE. A MESSENGER REACHED US THAT EVENING SAYING THAT MY FATHER WANTED US TO GO NORTH TO THE OTHER KINGDOMS AND GET HELP.

WE SET SAIL SECRETLY THAT NIGHT ACROSS THE RANN TO LAL DARO, YOUR GATEWAY FORT, ONLY TO FIND IT BURNING... ITS GARRISON DEAD OR DYING... THE AKKADIAN FLEET HAVING REACHED THERE BEFORE WE COULD.

IT WAS FROM A DYING SOLDIER THAT WE HEARD SOME TERRIFYING NEWS. THE AKKADIANS HAVE A SECRET WEAPON – A BLACK LIQUID – WHICH THEY KEEP IN BARRELS. THE BARRELS WERE ROLLED UP AGAINST THE FORT WALLS AND THEN SET ON FIRE.

THE BARRELS EXPLODED AND THE FORT WALLS FELL IN A CLOUD OF DUST. HE ALSO TOLD US THAT A LARGE FLEET OF AKKADIAN WARSHIPS HAD SAILED UP THE SINDHU RIVER AFTER THE FORT FELL. THIS WOULD HAVE BEEN FOUR DAYS AGO.

WE THEN RACED ALONG THE DRY BED OF THE NARA, AND AT YOUR BORDER, WERE MET BY YOUR FRONTIER GUARDS WHO BROUGHT US HERE.

A LITTLE LATER.

WHAT ARE THEY GOING TO DECIDE? WILL THEY HELP US? OR WILL THEY--

PRINCE, THESE THINGS ARE OUT OF OUR HANDS. WE SHOULD NOT WORRY. WE SHOULD JUST KEEP A CLEAR HEAD.

A FEW HOURS LATER

LORDS, THE WAR COUNCIL HAS FINISHED MEETING, AND I HAVE BEEN ASKED TO ESCORT YOU BACK TO THE AUDIENCE HALL.

PRINCE, BEFORE YOU CAME, WE WERE NOT SURE OF THE NATURE OF THE THREAT.

WE WERE NOT SURE WHETHER THE AKKADIAN ATTACKS ON OUR TOWNS WERE JUST TO KEEP US OCCUPIED WHILE THEY ATTACKED KUTCH, OR WHETHER IT WAS, AS WE FEARED, AN INVASION.

MY SPIES INFORM ME THAT SARGON HAS BEEN BOASTING IN HIS COURT THAT HE INTENDS TO RULE THE WORLD.

THE NEWS YOU BROUGHT ABOUT LAL DARO SUGGESTS THAT HE INTENDS TO START HIS EXPLOIT BY TAKING OVER OUR LANDS.

I AGREE WITH YOUR ASSESSMENT THAT TIME IS SHORT. I HAVE, THEREFORE, DECIDED THAT WE WILL MUSTER ALL OUR FORCES AND GET THEM READY FOR AN ALL OUT WAR.

I AGREE ENTIRELY WITH MY OLD FRIEND, YOUR FATHER, THAT THIS IS A BATTLE WE WILL ALL HAVE TO FIGHT TOGETHER IF WE HAVE TO WIN.

34

TO LAUNCH A SUCCESSFUL COUNTER ATTACK ON THE AKKADIANS, WE NEED TO GET THE MAXIMUM TROOPS HERE WITHIN THE NEXT TEN DAYS. BEYOND THAT, I DO NOT THINK THE GARRISON AT AMRI WILL BE ABLE TO HOLD THEM OUT.

MINISTER, SEND AN EMISSARY IMMEDIATELY TO GHANWERIWALA THER TO ASK THEIR KING TO SEND HIS ARMY.

HARAPPA, TOO, HAS A STRONG ARMY THAT CAN GET HERE IN NO TIME ON ITS LARGE FLEET OF SHIPS. BUT, UNFORTUNATELY, OUR KINGDOMS ARE NOT ON THE BEST TERMS CURRENTLY. PERHAPS YOU CAN HELP IN THIS REGARD?

LORD, I WILL BE HAPPY TO HELP YOU. I AM TO BE MARRIED TO PRINCESS KUNDALINI, DAUGHTER OF RAJA MAHAVINDASA, LORD OF HARAPPA, AND HAVE LONG HOPED FOR AN OPPORTUNITY TO VISIT.

GOOD. THEN WE SHALL MAKE ARRANGEMENTS FOR YOUR TRAVEL TO HARAPPA, AND I WILL ALSO HAVE RAJA MAHAVINDASA KNOW OF YOUR ARRIVAL. BUT BEFORE THAT, WILL YOU AND YOUR COMPANION PLEASE COME WITH ME?

PRINCE, THERE ARE A FEW THINGS I NEED TO DISCUSS WITH YOU IN PRIVATE AND AWAY FROM MY OWN COURT. PLEASE COME THIS WAY.

THESE ARE STRANGE TIMES, INDEED, THAT A KING FEELS FREE TO TALK ONLY IN THE PALACE'S GUEST CHAMBERS.

WHAT BOTHERS YOU, MY LORD?

ABOUT THREE MONTHS AGO, I WAS FORCED TO EXILE MY CHIEF MINISTER TAKSHAKA WHEN I DISCOVERED THAT HE WAS PLANNING TO OVERTHROW ME.

THE PROBLEM IS THAT I HAVE NOT BEEN ABLE TO UNCOVER ALL THE PEOPLE INVOLVED IN THE PLOT. I SUSPECT THAT SOME MAY STILL BE HERE IN THE CITY...

...AND SOME MAY STILL BE HERE IN THE PALACE. WE HAVE ALSO HEARD RUMOURS THAT TAKSHAKA IS NOW GUIDING THE INVADERS.

WHAT WOULD YOU HAVE US DO?

VERY WELL, MY LORD, WE WILL LEAVE WITH YOUR PERMISSION TWO SUNRISES FROM TODAY.

REST YOURSELVES NOW. I WILL SEND FOR THE GUARD TO TAKE YOU TO YOUR QUARTERS AND ARRANGE FOR SOME ENTERTAINMENT FOR TOMORROW NIGHT.

THANK YOU, YOUR HIGHNESS.

STAY HERE IN MY CITY FOR ONE MORE DAY, AND LET ME MAKE YOUR TRAVEL ARRANGEMENTS AS SECURE AS POSSIBLE. AFTER ALL, EVERYONE KNOWS YOU ARE IN MOHENJO-DARO AND WILL GO TO HARAPPA NEXT.

EXCELLENT. I WILL DEPUTE MY PERSONAL GUARD FOR YOUR PROTECTION.

36

THE NEXT MORNING.

CHANDRAYAAN, LET US GO AND SEE THIS CITY THAT YOU HAVE TOLD ME SO MUCH ABOUT OVER THE YEARS.

VERY WELL, BUT PLEASE REMEMBER TO STAY NEAR ME AND THE GUARDS. I REMEMBER TAKSHAKA WELL, AND HE IS VERY DANGEROUS.

AFTER BREAKFAST, PRINCE MELUHA AND CHANDRAYAAN, WITH THE KING'S PERMISSION AND TWO GUARDS, WENT TO SEE THE CITY.

LOOK AROUND AND LEARN, PRINCE. THIS CHAOS OF SO MANY THOUSANDS OF PEOPLE BUYING AND SELLING GOODS IS ACTUALLY MADE POSSIBLE BY A VERY EFFICIENT SYSTEM OF REGULATIONS.

YOU WILL NOT SEE ANY DELIVERY CARTS HERE. THERE ARE SPECIFIC TIMES SET FOR THE PICK UP AND DELIVERY OF GOODS, SO THE STREETS STAY CLEAR FOR SHOPPERS THE REST OF THE TIME. THE GARBAGE HAS TO BE CLEARED MANY TIMES A DAY BY A TEAM OF SWEEPERS.

LAPIZ BEADS!

YES, MY PRINCE. THEY ARE BROUGHT ALL THE WAY FROM ARIA. IMAGINE THE LONG TRADE NETWORKS THAT HAVE TO BE MADE AND CONTROLLED TO BRING THESE BEADS HERE, AFTER OVER A MONTH'S JOURNEY.

SEE THE SHELL BANGLES – THEY ARE FROM KUTCH. THEY PROBABLY PASSED THROUGH DHOLAVIRA ON THEIR WAY HERE.

LOOK AT THE VARIETY OF VEGETABLES. HAVE YOU EVER SEEN SO MANY TYPES OF GREEN LEAVES?

ARE THESE VEGETABLES LOCALLY PRODUCED IN THE FIELDS WE PASSED?

YES, WITHIN A DAY OR TWO'S WALK, AT THE MOST.

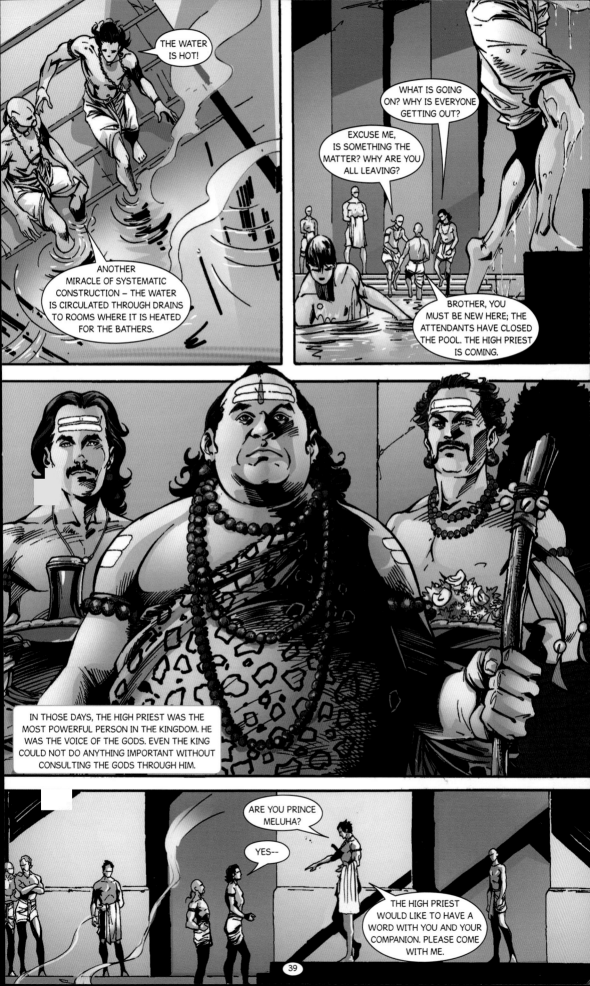

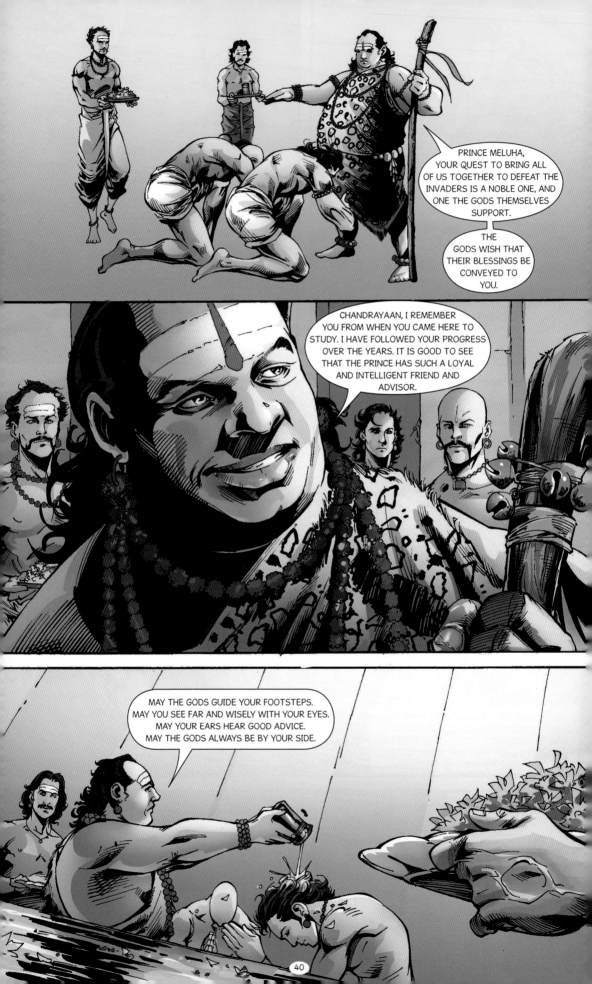

LORD, A DRINK OF THE FINEST AND MOST POTENT MAHUWA FROM THE TREES IN THE KING'S OWN GARDEN.
IN THE BEGINNING OF THE UNIVERSE, THE SKIES WERE ALWAYS DARK. PEOPLE FEARED FOR THEIR SAFETY AND BANDITS RULED THE ROADS AND FIELDS. IN SUCH TIMES, A PRINCESS SEARCHING FOR HER LOST LOVE PRAYED TO THE GODS TO LIGHT UP THE NIGHT.
THE GODS WERE MOVED BY HER PLEA, BUT THEY COULD NOT HELP HER BECAUSE THEY KNEW HER LOVER WAS DEAD. THEREFORE, THEY RAISED HER UP TO THE SKY TO BECOME...
THE MOON ITSELF AND LIGHT THE NIGHT SKY, SO THAT NO OTHER LOVERS COULD EVER BE SEPARATED AGAIN IN THE DARK.
EVEN TODAY, SHE IS UP THERE, WATCHING OVER THE NIGHT SKY... HER HOPES RISING AND DIMINISHING IN A CYCLE, AS SHE SEARCHES ON FOR HER LOST LOVE.
AAAAH! THE MAHUWA IS GOOD. DID YOU LIKE IT?
WAS IT? I WANT TO WAKE UP EARLY TOMORROW SO I DID NOT HAVE ANY.
PROBABLY A GOOD IDEA, BUT THE ATTENDANT WAS RIGHT. IT IS VERY STRONG.

COME ON, EVERYONE! CLEAR UP THE PLACE! DO YOU WANT TO STAY HERE ALL NIGHT? PICK UP AND CLEAN THOSE GLASSES, THEY BELONG TO THE PALACE.

AFTER THE PROGRAMME HAD ENDED, PRINCE MELUHA AND CHANDRAYAAN RETIRED TO THEIR ROOM.

AH! LOOKS LIKE THE PRINCE DIDN'T WANT ANY DRINK. NOW, IT IS MY TURN TO BE THE KING! I SHALL DRINK FROM A GOLDEN GLASS!

WHERE IS THAT MAN I SENT TO WASH THE GLASSES? THESE PEOPLE NEED A CHANCE TO ESCAPE WORK. I'LL TAKE HIM TO TASK WHEN I SEE HIM.

GUARDS! GUARDS!

WITHIN MINUTES, PANIC SPREAD. THE GUARDS RAN TO CALL THE CHIEF MINISTER TO TAKE CHARGE OF THE SITUATION.

I ASSUME THE GOLDEN GLASS WAS THE ONE THE PRINCE WAS MEANT TO DRINK FROM? THE DRINK WAS OBVIOUSLY POISONED.

SIR--

I WANT A LIST OF EVERYONE WHO WAS THERE – GUESTS, STAFF, AND ENTERTAINERS – IMMEDIATELY.

THE NEXT DAY.

A LOVELY MORNING AND A GOOD DAY TO START OUR JOURNEY TO HARAPPA.

YES, A LIGHT MEAL AND WE SHALL BE READY TO LEAVE.

HIS HIGHNESS HAS SENT ME TO REQUEST YOU TO REMAIN HERE AND NOT VENTURE OUT TILL HE COMES HIMSELF. HE WISHES TO SPEAK TO YOU IN PRIVATE.

AFTER SOME TIME, THE KING WALKED INTO PRINCE MELUHA'S ROOM WITHOUT ANY GUARD IN SIGHT.

SORRY FOR DETAINING YOU LIKE THIS, BUT SOMEONE TRIED TO KILL YOU LAST NIGHT.

WHAT!

THE GLASS OF MAHUWA THAT YOU WERE OFFERED DURING THE PROGRAMME WAS POISONED. THE CLEANER, WHO DRANK IT AFTERWARDS, WAS FOUND DEAD EARLY THIS MORNING.

I TOLD YOU ON A PREVIOUS OCCASION... TAKSHAKA HAS MANY FRIENDS.

I THINK WE CAN ASSUME THAT THE PLANS I MADE FOR YOUR JOURNEY TO HARAPPA ARE KNOWN TO HIM.

CAN OUR TRAVEL PLANS BE CHANGED?

NO. TIME IS SHORT AND, IN ANY CASE, I AM SURE TAKSHAKA'S SPIES WILL BE WATCHING.

WE WILL HAVE TO BE VIGILANT.

SO BE IT.

EACH OF THESE WARSHIPS CARRIES THIRTY OF MY BRAVEST GUARDS. THEY WILL ESCORT YOU ALL THE WAY TO HARAPPA.

I DO NOT KNOW HOW TO THANK YOU ENOUGH FOR--

JUST SUCCEED.

MY LORDS, HIS HIGHNESS HAS APPRISED ME OF THE GRAVITY OF THE SITUATION AND THE THREAT FACING US ALL. I HAVE, THEREFORE, DECIDED THAT WE HAD BEST STAY ON THE RIVER ITSELF AND NOT STOP ALONG THE SHORE EN ROUTE AS PLANNED.

WHEN WILL WE REACH?

AS YOU CAN SEE, OUR JOURNEY WILL TAKE US UP THE SINDHU TO THE JUNCTION WITH THE RIVER SUTLEJ. FROM THERE, A SHORT RIDE UP THE SUTLEJ WILL BRING US TO THE RIVER RAVI, AND THEN TO HARAPPA.

IF ALL GOES WELL AND THE WIND REMAINS STRONG AT OUR BACK, WE SHALL REACH HARAPPA TOMORROW EVENING.

BEAUTIFUL VIEW. I WOULD HAVE LOVED STOPPING HERE.

I WOULD NOT RECOMMEND IT. SEE OVER THERE... CAMELS!

I AM AFRAID RAJA SUSHANA WAS RIGHT... WE ARE BEING WATCHED.

TIME FOR SOME REST NOW.

THE NEXT MORNING, PRINCE MELUHA AND CHANDRAYAAN WOKE UP WITH A START.

CAPTAIN! EMERGENCY!

WE CANNOT LEAVE WITHOUT TAKING CARE OF THE DEAD.

WE WILL LOSE TIME IF--

WE **CANNOT** LEAVE THEM HERE, CAPTAIN, AND WE **WILL** NOT.

SEEING THE FIRMNESS IN PRINCE MELUHA'S VOICE, THE CAPTAIN IMMEDIATELY ORDERED HIS MEN TO START DIGGING GRAVES FOR THE DEAD.

HURRY UP! WE DON'T HAVE MUCH TIME IN HAND.

MOVE IT! MOVE IT!

CAPTAIN, PLEASE HAVE THE AKKADIAN DEAD ALSO GATHERED UP. WE WILL BURY THEM AS WELL.

BUT--

LET US RESPECT ALL THE DEAD, CAPTAIN.

SOME TIME LATER.

MY LORDS, OUR DEAD ARE IN THEIR GRAVES. WE HAVE ALSO BURIED THE ENEMY SOLDIERS IN A MASS GRAVE ON THE OTHER SIDE OF THE DUNE.

51

YOU DO NOT KNOW HOW HAPPY I WAS WHEN FATHER TOLD ME THAT MY FONDEST WISH WOULD BE COMING TRUE IN A FEW YEARS.

IF ONLY HE KNEW HOW MANY HINTS I DROPPED TO MY FATHER, UNTIL HE BEGAN TO THINK ABOUT MY MARRIAGE!

BUT ALL THAT WILL HAVE TO WAIT NOW. I AM NOT SURE IF YOU WILL WANT TO MARRY A PRINCE WITHOUT A KINGDOM?

HUSH! DO NOT TALK LIKE THAT. YOU KNOW I WILL ALWAYS STAND BY YOU.

WHEN THE ARMY LEAVES, I WILL BE COMING ALONG.

KUNDALINI, YOU CANNOT BE SERIOUS; IT IS VERY DANGEROUS OUT THERE RIGHT NOW.

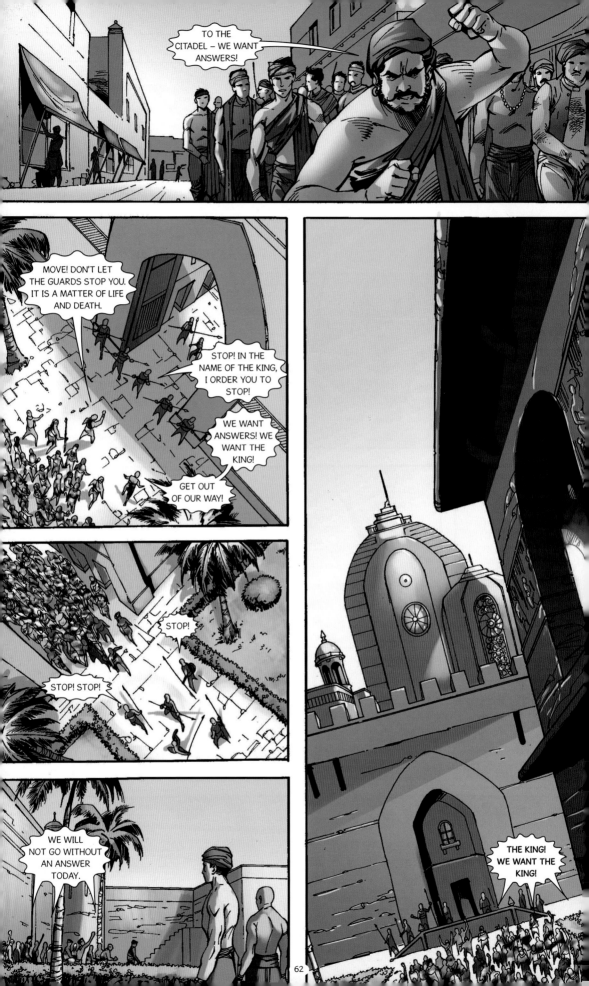

I AM SORRY... BUT IT IS TOO LATE NOW...

AND SO IT WAS THAT GOOD RAJA MAHAVINDASA, WHO HAD DEFEATED SO MANY ENEMIES ON THE BATTLEFIELD WITH HONOUR, DIED AT THE HANDS OF AN UNSEEN AND COWARDLY ASSASSIN.

LATER IN THE DAY, IN THE PRINCESS'S ROOM.

OH, WHY DID HE HAVE TO DIE? WHO WILL STOP THE INVADERS NOW?

PRINCESS, COME HERE! LET ME HOLD YOU AND COMFORT YOU.

THE ROYAL CEMETERY OF HARAPPA.

ALL GREAT RULERS IN THOSE DAYS WERE BURIED UNDER HIGH, CIRCULAR, MUD-BRICK BURIAL MOUNDS. IN THE CENTRE FAR BELOW, WERE LARGE STONE WALLED CRYPTS INTO WHICH THE BODY WOULD BE PLACED.

OFFERINGS OF FOOD AND DRINK FAVOURED BY THE DEAD KING WERE LOWERED DOWN TO EASE HIS JOURNEY INTO THE AFTERLIFE.

IN THOSE DAYS, GREAT PEOPLE WERE BURIED AND NOT CREMATED. CREMATION WAS RESERVED FOR COMMON PEOPLE AND PRIESTS.

AND SO, WITH THE SEALING OF THE CRYPT, THIS CHAPTER OF OUR STORY MUST END. GOING BACK TO THE WAR...

TWO DAYS LATER.

CAPTAIN MAASHI, THE QUEEN AND HER GUESTS WILL BE ARRIVING SHORTLY. HOW MUCH IS LEFT TO BE LOADED?

ALL THE EQUIPMENT AND STORES HAVE BEEN LOADED, GENERAL SIMHA. THE PERSONAL ITEMS OF THE QUEEN AND HER GUESTS ARE NOW BEING LOADED ON THE FLAGSHIP. WE SHOULD BE DONE BEFORE THEY REACH.

YOUR HIGHNESS, WE ARE READY TO DEPART ON YOUR COMMAND. YOUR PERSONAL ITEMS HAVE BEEN LOADED INTO YOUR CABIN.

VERY GOOD, GENERAL SIMHA, WHAT NEWS DO YOU HAVE OF THE FLEET AND ARMY?

YOUR HIGHNESS, THE ARMY BOARDED THE FLEET A FEW KILOMETRES DOWNSTREAM THIS MORNING, AND HAS ALREADY DEPARTED FOR SIND. AS PER YOUR INSTRUCTIONS, MINISTER AYASTU HAS LEFT WITH THEM. HE IS ALSO THE BEARER OF YOUR LETTER TO RAJA SUSHANA.

SO BEGINS THE SECOND HALF OF OUR JOURNEY. MAY THE GODS SMILE UPON US AND HELP US LIBERATE OUR PEOPLE.

MAY WE DEFEAT THEM IN SUCH A MANNER THAT NO ONE LOOKS THIS WAY AGAIN FOR A THOUSAND YEARS.

WITH A HEAVY HEART THE PRINCE, NOW ACCOMPANIED BY A QUEEN, SET OFF IN DEFENCE OF THE REALM.

74

THE CITY OF MOHENJO-DARO HAD OVER THE WEEK DOUBLED IN POPULATION, WITH TENS OF THOUSANDS OF SOLDIERS COMING IN FROM ALL CORNERS OF THE LAND. A GREAT ARMY OF A SIZE NOT SEEN IN MANY CENTURIES HAD BEGUN GATHERING.

WELCOME BACK, PRINCE MELUHA! LOOK AROUND YOU; YOUR CALL FOR HELP HAS BEEN ANSWERED.

IT WOULD NOT HAVE BEEN POSSIBLE WITHOUT YOUR HELP, BUT FIRST, MAY I INTRODUCE YOU TO QUEEN KUNDALINI, RULER OF HARAPPA.

QUEEN? BUT WHERE IS MAHAVINDASA, MY OLD FRIEND? I WAS EXPECTING HI--

HE IS NO MORE.

I AM SORRY TO HAVE TO TELL YOU THAT MY FATHER FELL TO AN ARROW FROM THE HANDS OF THAT TRAITOR, TAKSHAKA.

MY DEEPEST SYMPATHIES TO YOU, MY DEAR. I NOW DOUBLY REGRET THAT I ONLY EXILED THAT EVIL SERPENT INSTEAD OF HAVING HIM KILLED.

COME WITH ME TO MY PALACE. WE HAVE MUCH TO DISCUSS AND THESE MUST BE HELD IN PRIVATE. THERE ARE MANY IN MY CITY WHOSE ALLEGIANCE I DOUBT.

76

LATER IN THE KING'S PRIVATE MEETING ROOM.

THE AKKADIAN ARMY IS STILL BEING HELD AT AMRI. OUR FORCES WILL BE AT FULL STRENGTH AND READY FOR ACTION IN A WEEK.

I HAVE DISCUSSED IT WITH MY GENERALS AND AM PLANNING A THREE-PRONGED ATTACK TO TRAP THE ENEMY AND WIPE THEM OUT.

WITH YOUR PERMISSION, I WOULD LIKE TO SUGGEST AN ALTERNATIVE PLAN WHICH, IF IT WORKS, WILL WIN US THIS WAR WITHOUT MUCH FIGHTING.

IS THE DANCING GIRLS' TROUPE LEADER STILL IN YOUR CUSTODY?

YES. WE HAVE NOT FOUND ANY PROOF AGAINST HER, BUT I WAS NOT GOING TO RELEASE HER WITH YOU TWO HERE.

CAN YOU HAVE HER BROUGHT HERE? I WOULD LIKE TO TALK TO HER.

GUARD! HAVE THAT DANCER BROUGHT HERE IMMEDIATELY!

AMAZING! YOU COULD BE MY TWIN.

I WOULD LIKE TO GIVE YOU AN OPPORTUNITY TO PROVE YOUR INNOCENCE.

I AM INNOCENT. WHAT DO YOU WANT ME TO DO?

I NEED YOU TO PRETEND TO BE KUNDALINI AND EXPOSE YOURSELF IN SUCH A MANNER THAT THE ENEMY TRIES TO CAPTURE YOU, THINKING THAT YOU ARE THE QUEEN.

THE NEXT MORNING.

I HAVE CALLED ALL OF YOU HERE TO TELL YOU THAT WE WILL BE MARCHING IN A WEEK'S TIME. OUR FORCES ARE READY.

EVEN THOUGH WE VASTLY OUTNUMBER OUR ENEMY, THIS IS GOING TO BE A TOUGH FIGHT. I WOULD LIKE TO ASK YOU ALL TO ORGANISE PRAYERS FOR THE GODS. MAY THEY BLESS US ALL.

MY QUEEN!
WHAT! YOU TRICKED ME! GUARDS! GUARDS!
YOUR GUARDS ARE DEAD. MY ARMY IS HERE. SURRENDER, OR DIE!
KNOWING THAT EMPEROR SARGON WAS NOT KNOWN TO TAKE DEFEAT HAPPILY, AND THAT HE WOULD BE KILLED FOR FAILURE, ADMIRAL LUGABANDU STABBED HIMSELF TO DEATH.

A LITTLE LATER ON THE RIVERBANK.

CAPTAIN, TAKE THE BODY OF YOUR COMMANDER BACK TO SARGON WITH YOU. TELL YOUR SOLDIERS THAT YOU MEET ALONG THE WAY THAT THEY HAVE THREE SUNSETS FROM NOW TO LEAVE OUR LANDS, OR I WILL KILL THEM ALL!

TELL THEM THAT EVEN NOW AN ARMY SO LARGE THAT ITS FOOTSTEPS KICK UP DUST ENOUGH TO DIM THE SUN AND MAKE THE EARTH TREMBLE IS MARCHING TOWARDS THEM!

TELL THEM TO LEAVE NOW OR NEVER SEE THEIR FAMILIES AGAIN. TELL THEM THEY WILL SOON BE THE FOOD OF THE VULTURES AND WILD ANIMALS OF OUR LANDS! LEAVE NOW!

I MUST ADMIT, I DID NOT BELIEVE YOUR PLAN WOULD SUCCEED.

THE GODS AND A BIT OF LUCK WERE ON OUR SIDE.

DO YOU THINK THEY WILL LEAVE NOW THAT THE ADMIRAL IS DEAD?

HARD TO SAY, BUT WE WILL KEEP OUR WORD AND ADVANCE ONLY AFTER TWO DAYS. IN THE MEANTIME, WE WILL RETURN TO MOHENJO-DARO, WHILE SOME SHIPS WILL SAIL DOWN THE RIVER TO KEEP AN EYE ON THE ENEMY.

AND SO IT WAS FIVE DAYS AFTER RAJA SUSHANA'S ULTIMATUM THAT A FLAGSHIP BEARING THE PRINCE AND THE QUEEN ARRIVED AT DHOLAVIRA, THE AKKADIAN ARMY HAVING WITHDRAWN AND LEFT TO RETURN TO AKKAD.

FATHER! MOTHER!

WELCOME HOME, SON!

I KNEW YOU HAD SUCCEEDED WHEN THE ENEMY LEFT THREE DAYS AGO, EVEN WHEN THEY WERE ON THE VERGE OF VICTORY.

GOD BLESS YOU AND WELCOME HOME, MY CHILDREN.

FATHER, I WOULD LIKE YOU TO MEET THE YOUNG LADY YOU HAD CHOSEN FOR ME – KUNDALINI – NOW A QUEEN.

93

A WEEK LATER, RAJA SANJAYA WAS JOINED BY RAJA SUSHANA TO CELEBRATE THEIR VICTORY OVER SARGON'S FORCES.

MANY WEEKS AGO, BEFORE THE ENEMY ATTACKED, I TOLD YOU THAT I WOULD STEP DOWN WHEN MY SON AND YOUR PRINCE WAS READY.

AFTER HEARING WHAT MY GOOD FRIEND RAJA SUSHANA HAS TO SAY ABOUT PRINCE MELUHA'S CONDUCT, I KNOW THAT THE TIME HAS COME FOR ME...

...TO HAND OVER THE CROWN TO HIM. MAY HIS RULE BE JUST AND WISE.

THANK YOU, FATHER.

TOMORROW SHALL BE A GREAT DAY; WE SHALL FIRST ANOINT OUR NEW KING AND THEN MARRY OUR KING TO HIS QUEEN!

MAY THE GODS BLESS THIS UNION OF TWO INDIVIDUALS AND TWO KINGDOMS. MAY PROSPERITY ALWAYS REIGN.

THE NEXT DAY.

OH RAJA SANJAYA, YOU HAVE RULED US WISELY FOR SO MANY YEARS. ON BEHALF OF THE GODS, I RECEIVE THIS CROWN, FREELY GIVEN, TO PASS ON TO YOUR WORTHY SUCCESSOR.

TODAY, ON THIS AUSPICIOUS DAY, I CALL ON YOU, FIRE, TO CARRY THESE OFFERINGS TO THE GODS AND ASK THEM TO COME HERE AND BLESS THIS DAY.

IN THE NAME OF THE GODS, I SEAT YOU ON THE THRONE OF DHOLAVIRA. ALL RISE FOR RAJA MELUHA!

A LITTLE LATER.

COME SON, IT IS TIME FOR YOU TO MARRY THE YOUNG LADY, WHO YOU TRIED SO HARD TO CONVINCE ME, WAS PERFECT FOR YOU.

I NOW PRONOUNCE YOU HUSBAND AND WIFE. MAY YOU LIVE HAPPILY EVER AFTER.

AND SO IT WAS THAT RAJA MELUHA AND QUEEN KUNDALINI, WHOM WE REMEMBER FOR LATER UNITING AND WISELY RULING THE ENTIRE HARAPPAN REALM, BECAME KING AND QUEEN AFTER DEFEATING A GREAT FOE WITH JUST A FEW SOLDIERS.

THEREFORE, MY YOUNG STUDENTS, I WANT YOU TO UNDERSTAND THAT WAR IS NOT THE ONLY SOLUTION TO A CONFLICT. TACT CAN WIN KINGDOMS WITHOUT MUCH LOSS OF BLOOD.

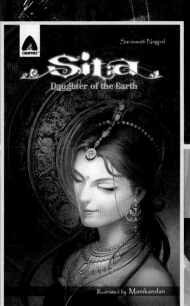

Sita

Daughter of the Earth

Written by Saraswati Nagpal
Illustrated by Manikandan

Adapted from the ancient Indian epic, the *Ramayana*, this is a rare, first-person account of the fascinating story of one of the most iconic figures in Indian mythology.

CAMPFIRE™

www.campfire.co.in

www.campfire.co.in

Twisting between crime, time, mystery, and history, *Photo Booth* **is an intriguing thriller that will keep you hooked till the last page!**

He wanted to change the past, but first he would have to alter the future...

A new deadly drug is about to flood the streets of New York City. The police has no leads on who is producing the drug, or where it is coming from. As far as Praveer Rajani, a ruthless Interpol agent, is concerned, the only way to prevent countless deaths lies in a handful of mysterious photographs.

In the photographs, Praveer can see images of places he has never known, and people he has long forgotten. But what are the photographs leading him to? Is Praveer being told that his life is spiralling out of control, and he now has one chance to put things right?

Or are the photographs related to a murder that Praveer is desperate to solve? Perhaps they are showing the love that his brother, Jayendra, let slip away or even the family that his sister, Nisha, wants back.

The mystery will finally be solved in this exciting romantic thriller from Campfire.

GLOSSARY

Akkad: A lost ancient city, believed to lie in central Iraq, which was once the capital of a large empire founded by Sargon. It was also known as Agade.

Alexander: The Greek King Alexander the Great (356 BC–323 BC) invaded India in 326 BC and fought many battles with the tribes and kingdoms of western India.

Amri: An ancient city in the southern province of Sind, Pakistan, that existed from 3500 BC to 1500 BC.

Aria: An ancient name for the land of Ariana in Afghanistan.

Ashram: A retreat centre used by ascetics to meditate or teach pupils.

Citadel: Many of the large Indus towns and cities have elevated mounds or divisions with their own fortification, which are referred to as citadels by archaeologists.

Dholavira: Located on Khadir Island in Kutch, India, this ancient city was inhabited from 3100 BC to 1500 BC. It was one of the five largest Indus cities.

Dhruva: The ancient Indian name (popularly used now) for the star Thuban – the second last star in the tail of the constellation Ursa Major.

Dilmun: The ancient name of the island of Baharain. It was a major trading port and an ancient Mesopotamian cemetery.

Ganweriwala Ther: Located in the Cholistan Desert of Pakistan, this ancient city was inhabited from c.3100 BC to 2000 BC. It was one of the five largest Harappan cities, and once lay on the delta of the River Saraswati (modern River Ghaggar/Hara) where it met a large lake.

God Ea: Mesopotamian god of the Wind and Earth.

Goddess Aditi: Indian goddess of the Earth; Mother Earth.

Harappa: Located on the banks of the River Ravi in the province of Punjab in Pakistan, it was one of the most famous and largest Indus cities that has been extensively excavated. It existed from from c.3500 BC to 1700 BC.

Harappans: A name often applied to the people of the Indus Valley Civilisation, which existed from 2550 BC to 1950 BC. Archaeologists believe its ancient name may have been Meluha.

Kutch: The island district of Gujarat, India. It was once said to have been made up of seven islands. It was colonised by people from Sind around 3100 BC.

Lal Daro: An ancient town and fortified outpost, that lies within the delta of the River Indus. It gets its name, which means 'Red Mound', from the burnt red mud bricks that it is made up of.

Magan: The ancient land on both sides of the entrance to the Persian Gulf. It includes the UAE, northern Oman, and parts of the Makran Coast of Iran and Pakistan. It was a major source of copper during those times.

Mahuwa: A tree growing extensively in parts of western India from which a strong liquor is made.

Malwa: A high plateau in central India crisscrossed by many rivers. Today, most of this plateau is part of the Indian state of Madhya Pradesh.

Mohenjo-daro: Located on the banks of the River Indus in the Sind province, Pakistan, it was one of the most famous and largest Indus cities, and has been extensively excavated. It was founded sometime before 3100 BC and existed till 2000 BC, when it was abandoned. It was later reoccupied briefly during Buddhist times when a stupa and monastery were built on its citadel mound.

Naphtha: An ancient Greek term for the oil that used to ooze out of the ground in parts of the Middle East.

Pashupati: An ancient Indian god, probably tribal in origin. He is the 'Protector of Cattle' and is today another name for the Hindu god, Shiva.

Raja Rai Por (Porus): The ruler of a kingdom between the rivers Chenab and Jhelum in modern Punjab Province, Pakistan. He fought a famous battle with Alexander the Great in 326 BC, in which he lost.

Rakhigarhi: Located in the state of Haryana in India, it was one of the five largest Indus cities. It was occupied from c.3500 BC to 2000 BC.

Rann of Kutch: This extensive salt pan, which becomes a shallow sea during the monsoon, separates Kutch from the Sind province. It was once a shallow, navigable sea.

River Nara: A dry river channel that runs parallel and to the east of the River Indus in Sind, Pakistan. It is believed to either mark an ancient eastern course of the River Indus or the channel of the River Saraswati.

River Ravi: This is one of the tributaries of the River Indus. The city of Harappa lies on its banks.

River Sutlej: A tributary of the River Indus.

River Sindhu: The ancient name of the modern River Indus.

Sapta Rishi: The Indian name for the constellation of Ursa Major, or the Big Dipper.

Saran: A fortified outpost on the northern shore of Khadir Island, about two kilometres from Dholavira.

Sargon: The greatest ruler of the ancient city of Akkad, Sargon lived from 2334 BC to 2279 BC. He was known as Sargon the Great, and vastly expanded the Akkadian Empire.

Shishupala: The Indian name for the constellation Ursa Minor, or the Little Dipper.

Sind: The southern province of modern Pakistan through which the River Indus flows.

Varanasi: A holy city located in central India.

Zebu Bull: A variety of *Bos indicus*, the type of cattle common throughout India.

THE CIVILISATION THAT WAS

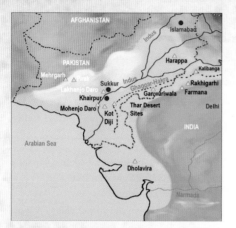

Almost 4000 years ago, when most cultures consisted of nomadic forest dwellers, a great civilisation, which can boast of the earliest known accounts of urban planning, developed along the River Indus in the Indian subcontinent. It is known as the Indus Valley Civilisation. Its two great cities were Harappa and Mohenjo-daro. Let's find out some more fascinating information about them.

HOW THEY LIVED

The people of this civilisation lived in well-planned cities. Their houses were built of mud bricks, burnt bricks, and chiselled stones. Each house had a courtyard, a private well, and a bathroom. Some cities had large public baths that were generally used for religious bathing. The most famous one is the Great Bath in Mohenjo-daro. In many places, citadels were built. Carved stone gateways and fortified walls surrounded them. The citadels also had a huge range of water reservoirs around them.

THEIR JEWELLERY

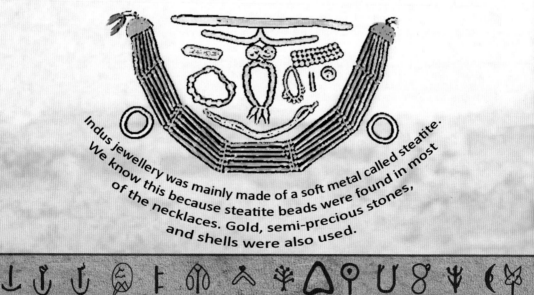

Indus jewellery was mainly made of a soft metal called steatite. We know this because steatite beads were found in most of the necklaces. Gold, semi-precious stones, and shells were also used.

THE PUZZLING DISCOVERIES

The River Indus used to flood regularly. When it did, cities in the Indus Valley Civilisation were rebuilt on top of the ones destroyed. Archaeologists have discovered several such rebuilt cities. However, what is puzzling is that each of the later cities were built a little less skillfully. The most well-planned and skillful one was at the bottom. Seems like builders grew less able in perfection over time!

Though the Indus Valley is the largest of all the four ancient civilisations (Egyptian, Mesopotamian, and Chinese being the other three), very little is known about it. Archaeologists have found four hundred distinct symbols on many well-carved seals. The seals bear carvings of animals, figures, and symbols of religious life along with a script that archaeologists have not been able to decipher. The seals may have been used in trade as many of them have been discovered in Mesopotamian sites. Till the time a Rosetta stone is found, discovering more information about this civilisation would be really tricky.

WHAT IS 'ROSETTA STONE'?

The Rosetta stone is an ancient Egyptian artefact that helped understand Egyptian hieroglyphics (a formal writing system used by ancient Egyptians). It is made of black basalt stone and was found in 1799. Though discovered by a soldier of the French Expedition to Egypt, the Rosetta stone came into British possession when the British troops defeated the French in 1801. It is the most visited object in the British Museum. The term 'Rosetta stone' also means a clue, breakthrough, or discovery that provides crucial knowledge for solving a problem.

DID YOU KNOW?

- The name 'India' has been derived from the River Indus, the valleys around which were the home of the early settlers of the Indus Valley Civilisation.

- Sindhu is the ancient name of the River Indus.

- The Indus Valley Civilisation is also known as the Harappan, Indus-Saraswati, and Hakra Civilisation.

Available now

Putting the fun back into reading!

Explore the latest from Campfire at

www.campfire.co.in